Irene Winnard

A Life of Miracles

Hiram LeMay

Copyright © 2012 by Hiram LeMay.

All rights reserved. No part of this book may be used or reproduced by any means, graphic, electronic, or mechanical, including photocopying, recording, taping or by any information storage retrieval system without the written permission of the publisher except in the case of brief quotations embodied in critical articles and reviews.

WestBow Press books may be ordered through booksellers or by contacting:

WestBow Press
A Division of Thomas Nelson
1663 Liberty Drive
Bloomington, IN 47403
www.westbowpress.com
1-(866) 928-1240

Because of the dynamic nature of the Internet, any web addresses or links contained in this book may have changed since publication and may no longer be valid. The views expressed in this work are solely those of the author and do not necessarily reflect the views of the publisher, and the publisher hereby disclaims any responsibility for them.

Any people depicted in stock imagery provided by Thinkstock are models, and such images are being used for illustrative purposes only.

Certain stock imagery © Thinkstock.

ISBN: 978-1-4497-3984-3 (sc)

Library of Congress Control Number: 2012902235

Printed in the United States of America

WestBow Press rev. date: 02/13/2012

Dedicated to my wife Jessie Hearn LeMay

Acknowledgments

It is hard to find words to express my deepest appreciation to the wonderful people who have been so kind to give the help that I have needed in putting my life story together.

It would not have been possible without the time that my dear friend Mrs. Linda Winn has given so freely. I really don't know how to say thanks to her and Ryan White for the time they spent helping me with the computer. But one thing is for sure, I will always hold you both dear to me. You may not know this, but you both were an answer to prayer.

Introduction

To God Be The Glory

> In all thy ways acknowledge Him, and He shall direct thy paths.
> (Proverbs: 3:6 KJV)

I am now 87 years old and soon will be 88 if all goes well until July 31, 2012. I thought it was time for me to write my life story for my precious family: five children, 11 grandchildren, 16 great-grandchildren, and my wonderful wife Jessie Hearn LeMay who continues to be a precious wife to me.

None of this would be possible if it had not been for the blessings received from my wonderful Savior and Lord. He gave me the privilege of becoming a child of God at the age of 25 and the leadership of the sweet Holy Spirit to guide me in all my decisions. It has always been and will continue to be my earnest prayer, until God opens the windows of heaven and calls me home, that all of my family and loved ones will meet me there. Many of the things were hard to write about, but I felt someone someday might receive a blessing by knowing some things that they would have never known.

My life story will include remarks about my birth and my family; some unpleasant things and some funny things; events and friends from early childhood; my romantic and married life; army life; my poetry, hobbies, and sports interests; and all phases of my ministry including God's calling, churches I served, revivals, and my work with the Tennessee Baptist convention and the Southern Baptist convention.

My parents
Charles Wesley LeMay Sr. and
Gertrude Morgan LeMay

Hiram LeMay
Born July 31, 1924

My Family

Life had it's beginning July 31, 1924 in Memphis, Tennessee when Gertrude Morgan LeMay gave birth to an 11 pound 6 ounce baby boy named Hiram Alexander LeMay. I was named after my two grandfathers: my father's dad was named Hiram, and my mother's dad was named Alexander.

I was the third child. Charles Wesley Le May Jr. was the first born, and Frances was the second. Following at two year intervals: Laverne, Robert Edward, Jack Collins, and James Albert were added to the family making a total of seven children. Two girls and five boys. It is very easy to see that Charles Wesley LeMay Sr. and Gertrude LeMay had their work laid out for them as times were very hard just on the heels of a great depression.

My dad worked for the Missouri Pacific Railroad where he worked six days a week up until the time he took early retirement because of heart problems. Dad died at the age of 69 when his heart gave away in 1970. He was buried in Forest Hills Cemetery in Memphis. Before dad's death, he was a very active and very kind person. I remember times when he would bring people into our house, give them something to eat, and let them sleep inside on a blanket on the floor to stay out of the freezing weather.

Dad was also very talented. He could play almost any kind of musical instrument, and he was a good singer. He led the Missouri Pacific Minstrel Show for several years as shown here. Several of our family also helped in different ways. Charles, Laverne and her husband Robert Comer, and Jack and myself would play and sing at some of the shows.

On one occasion Dad invented a tool to aid in doing the job that he had with the railroad and sold his invention to the company for $ 350.00. At that time he thought that was a lot of money but found out later that he could have sold it for much more. The money was used to buy our first auto—a T Model Ford. Boy were we proud.

One day Dad road to work with another man, and mother thought she would take a chance at driving. She ran the car through the garage causing small damage to the car, but the crash was too much for the old shed. It fell apart. We knew that trouble was just ahead when Dad came home from work, but lucky enough he just laughed it off.

Time moved on in our family, and Dad gave in to the pressures of the day. He started drinking alcohol until it became a real problem in our family life. There had been such a change in Dad and his activities that we very seldom saw him sober. He spent most of his nights at one of the local beer joints and sometimes he went as far as Tunica, Mississippi to play music and drink alcohol. They would furnish him all he could drink, and many times he would come home late at night very drunk and would be mean to Mother and anyone who would try to help Mother.

On one occasion my brother tried to keep Dad from sticking Mother with his knife, and the knife went through my brothers hand. When Dad saw the blood it seemed to make him sick, and he fell back in his chair and began to cry. Of course we were all busy trying to minister help to our brother.

It was not very long after this tragedy that Mother said to me, "We need to go down to the honky tonk and get your Dad so he will be able to go to work in morning." We left and went to the honky tonk. Dad came out and started walking with us up the road. We had not gone very far until Dad turned around and hit Mother in the face with the guitar and broke out several of her teeth. We were in front of a friend's house, and he came out to see what was going on. He picked Mother up, put her in his car, and took her to the hospital. Dad ran back in the direction of the honky tonk.

After we returned from the hospital, we called our Uncle Newman Jones in Dyersburg, Tennessee to come and help us. He drove down, came in the house, and was there when Dad came home. He met Dad at the front door pulled him in the house and knocked him to the floor. Dad reached in his pocket to take out his switch blade knife, and uncle Newman said, "Go ahead and take it out, and I will use it to cut your head off."

Of course, you know he never took it out. We gave Dad some black coffee, set him up in a chair, and Uncle Newman gave him a lecture. He said if he ever had to come back again because of this type of treatment, Dad would not be able to do that again. Well as time went on it was several years before another occasion called for action.

My older brother and I decided we were big enough to take care of him this time. We talked it over and decided to fix up a trap for him when he returned home drunk from the honky tonk, and our plan worked.

Charles got in the sink by the back door with a stick of wood from behind the cook stove, and I grabbed a stick and got under the sink. When Dad came in around 12 o'clock, he pushed opened the back door that had no locks and stepped inside. Charlie hit him on the head, and I hit him across his legs. When he fell to the floor, we tied him up with a well rope, and dragged him to the couch in the living room. We gave him some black coffee, and he soon sobered up, and said he was sorry for what he had done, and said it would never happen again. You guessed it.

He never came home again drunk. At the age of 56, he became a Christian, joined the Church, and became a leader of the Men's Fellowship. He and Mother had 13 years of wonderful relationship before his death in 1970. I know very little about Mother's family, but I do know that she had two sisters, and one brother.

Louise was the oldest. She married Robert Branson, but gave up her marriage to move to Washington to work as a secretary in the White House. Her husband died a few years later. Mother said he died of a broken heart, as he loved Louise so much.

Uncle Earl never married and spent most of his life looking for the Lost Dutchman. He came home on one occasion and tried to get some of us to go back with him, but no one was interested. He died a few years later.

Aunt Bertha was the youngest, and Granny, who I never had the privilege of seeing, died in child birth with Bertha. Aunt Bertha was married to Newman Jones, and they had two sons, Skipper and Johnny. They lived in Dyersburg, Tennessee where Uncle Newman owned a Ford Motor Company. Their family was very good to us and helped us in many ways through our hard times.

Hiram LeMay

~~~~~~~

Moving on from those things that brought our family much sorrow to other experiences that were far more pleasant. I do hope that someone might read the unpleasant, and decide never to make the unwise decisions that Dad made that caused our family so many problems.

Well, we have already mentioned Mothers experience with the Model T Ford, and it was a very funny experience, but there was the task of replacing the old garage and removing a few dents from the Model T and put all back in good shape. Mother's driving experience caused her to never try her luck again. However there were some other things that brought laughter into our life.

One morning Mom went out to the chicken house to gather the eggs. Remember that Mom was only four feet six inches tall, and the chicken house, cow shed, and garden were all fenced in by a five foot fence. Well Mom had on her apron that had a little pocket in the front where she carried the eggs. Our milk machine Mary—our wonderful Jersey Cow—was not in a good mood, and she dropped her head made a snort and took out after Mom. This is for "Believe It Or Not." Mom ran to the fence, looked back, and saw Mary coming full speed, and knew she didn't have time to open the gate. Well would you believe she jumped flat footed over the five foot fence and didn't break one egg. All of kids were watching, holding our breath that she would get out of there before Mary could reach her. Well she did.

Most of the children today have fun in many different ways, but nothing like the kind that we had. I call it "home spun comedy." Mom was as stout as a young bull, and we found this out when we would do something wrong, like say a bad word. She would get us down in the floor, put her knee in our belly, push in, and stick a caster oil bottle in our mouth, pull her knee out, and make us swallow the whole thing. Of course we stayed too busy visiting the outhouse, better known as the "privy" to get in trouble of any kind for quite some time.

Having no TV, radio, telephone, or I-pod, made all our entertainment in our younger years come from everyday experiences such as the one just mentioned. I feel sure that most of the children today would have thought it to be real fun to watch mother as she would take the old red rooster by the neck, make about three powerful turns of her arm around and around, and end up with the rooster head in her hand, and the rooster flopping on the ground. When he flopped his last flop, she would tie his feet together and hang him up on the close line to drain, but the best part would come when she put him on the table with all the trimmings around him.

~~~~~~~~

Now that we have experienced some of the sad and some of the funny things that happened with Mother and Dad, let us move on to some of the things about the other members of our family.

Charles was the oldest and he was married to Alice Socker. They had three girls; Sandy who is married to Larry Miller. They live in Columbus, Indiana. Their second daughter was Jennie. She was in an auto accident returning home from a New Year's Party with her soon-to-be husband. They both were found in a roadside creek under their car. Of course they both lost their lives. I remember so well making the trip to Indiana for the funeral in freezing weather with ice and snow covered roads. We almost had a wreck as our car slid out of control, but the good Lord must have been with us. We did not hit another car but stopped against a curb and sat there for a few minutes to get our thinking straight and then went on our slippery way. Their third child was named Carol. She is married to a man named Watson. They also live in Indiana.

Charles was a preacher, and pastored several churches in Tennessee and one in Melton, Indiana. Charles and I both graduated from Belmont College in 1954. Charles went on to Southern Seminary but did not stay there very long. He started going to prayer meetings with a group that were strange in their beliefs, and he soon became attached to one of the women in the group and left his family. He and Alice got a divorce. Soon after the divorce, he joined up with some other preacher and moved to South America to start a mission there in Columbia. He was flying a plane with a family of eight and all were blind. The plane crashed in a mountain filled with underbrush, and the plane was not found until seven years later. Of course they were dead.

Frances was the second child, and she married William Phelps. They had three daughters. April, Susan, and Debbie. They are all married but I do not know their husbands' names. I know that Susan has a daughter named Jessica that spent a lot of time at mother's house after Dad passed away. Frances divorced Billy as he was going with another women. She later remarried and did not live very long. She died of kidney failure.

Let's just keep moving on through our family as best we can remember. I will skip over my own life for this time and move on to the fourth child. Bertha Laverne was married to Robert "Shorty" Comer. They had three children: Cathy, Johnny, and Eddie. All three were married. Cathy has died; and Laverne and Shorty are both dead. Laverne was a Sunday School teacher, and Shorty was Chairman of Deacons at Rugby Hills Baptist when I went there as Pastor in1960. They both played music and helped Dad in the Minstrel Show for several years. Shorty received Jesus as his Saviour in the first revival service that I preached in 1947. They were devoted to their church at Rugby Hills where they served until they died. Laverne was in very bad health and could not attend in the last few years of her life.

Jack Collins LeMay was the fifth child, and was married to Joe Ann Beavers, they had five girls I believe, but not sure. The oldest was Marilyn Jo, then Donna Jo. I'm not sure, but I think the next was Brenda Jo, and then Betty Jo, and finally Linda Jo. Jack never play an instrument, but when we would play music at home he would get two spoons and make music with them or slap his legs with his hand and make a sound in time with the song. I have known him to use a cigarette paper and hair comb to make music. Jack and JoAnn are both dead.

The sixth child was Robert Edward LeMay. He is married to Jo Ann LeMay. They have two girls and one adopted son. Mildred Ann was their first; then Harriet who has died, and Charlie is the son. Robert accepted God's call to preach, graduated for Harrison Chilhowee sometime in the '50's, and has been preaching as pastor in Tennessee churches ever since. At the age of 82 he is still a pastor of a Baptist Church. Robert has learned the art of chalk drawing and has been called upon through the years to give his chalk message to several churches.

Jimmy is the last of the LeMay Children. He is married to sweet lady named Jean. Jimmy has had several marriages. Some of his wives died. Other marriages ended in divorce. Jimmy is very talented in music and has written several songs and played in many clubs through the years. Since he married Jean, his writing has changed from country to Gospel, and he sings in churches. He put music to a poem that I wrote, "I Saw God this Morning" and had it copyrighted. He and Jean live in Jamestown, Wisconsin and are very happy. He has one daughter who lives in England named Katy.

My Childhood

Ages 1-8

During the days just following a great depression, there was never enough money for even the necessities of life for a family of seven children. I can well remember many cold winter days when we went out to catch the school bus with no jacket to wear, our noses running, and our feet freezing. Although Mother tried to send us looking as good as possible, this had some bad effects on my school life. I had an inferiority complex because of my lack of good clothes to wear. Fashion has changed so much that now kids wear blue jeans that have patches or holes in them, and the boys wear pants that drag the ground. It's a good thing they don't have to climb fences. They would get hung on the top wire. Standing before the class without any shoes on was very hard. I would rather stand in the corner with the dunce cap on my head. I guess all this got started very early in my life, as I was told in later life that I did not speak a word until I was three years old. I would grunt and point for things that I wanted.

Here I am sitting in a little car

My family told me that I was so fat they had to cut the sides out of the little car to get me out. This of course didn't have anything to do with the complex, but many other reasons did.

I was sick so often in the first grade that I missed enough school that I had to stay two years in the first grade. This added to the problem of Dad's drinking and Mother's staying so busy keeping the house, washing the clothes in an old iron kettle over a fire in the back yard, rinsing them in a number three wash tub, and hanging them on a solar dryer (better known as a close line that was stretched from the garage to the outhouse). When the clothes were dried, she took them to the ironing board which was a board laid across the backs of two kitchen table chairs behind our pot bellied stove on which she heated the iron. I can remember on many nights seeing my Mother ironing when we went to bed and still there when we got up to go to school. She did this so we would have clean clothes to wear. Even though they were not the very best, they would always be clean.

~~~~~~~~

There were many tasks to be performed with keeping seven children going, and all of us tried to do what we could the best we knew how. The girls helped with the house work and the boys stayed busy on the outside. We pumped water from the old hand pump in the back yard that produced water that looked like orange juice and had to be strained through a cloth to catch the iron rust. If we wanted good water to drink we had to walk about one half mile to the community spring or ask our neighbor if we could draw water from his well. We could only go when he was home as he had a pit bull tied to the well. He was not friendly at all.

Having two stoves to keep burning for cooking and heating kept my older brother and me busy most of the time pulling a cross cut saw through the logs we had brought in from the nearby woods. After we sawed the logs, we had to split them with a hand ax to make them the right size for the stove. Every morning before school one of us had the fun of milking Mary, the cow. That was not a very easy task, as Mary would often swish her tail across your face and raise her foot to stick it in the bucket held between your knees.

We would then take the milk into the house and put it in the ice box to get it good and cold so we could enjoy a good glass of milk and some of Mother's good cookies. Mary gave about six gallons of milk a day, but none ever lasted until the next day. What we did not drink, Mother would use in cooking or set it aside to let it clabber so we could all take turns at the churn to make our butter. There was nothing any better than Mother's biscuits with that good home-made butter, wild plum jelly, and a glass of Mary's milk with cream on the top. That is making me so hungry, I think I will go see what I can find to eat. I'll be right back.

~~~~~~~~

Well after one full day, we took turns visiting the one-hole privy, which was not much fun in the winter time. For the cleanup job, we had to use newspaper as the store-bought kind was too high as it cost two for a nickel. We would then come into our two bedroom house, stuff paper in the cracks of the windows to keep out the cold winter wind, bring in wood for the pot belly stove, fire it up real good, sit around until bed time listening to Dad and his friends play music or get in a corner of the room and study our lesson for school the next day.

The conditions in our house made it very hard for us to have any privacy at all as we only had two bedrooms, a very small living room with a couch that had bad springs, one lounge chair, and of course the pot belly stove with the box for the wood in back of the stove. This left only a very small area for the little children to play on the floor, and that is the reason the couch springs were all broken. The only thing to do in that small space was to jump up and down on the couch. Many times Mother would shout out, "Get off the couch!" But the jumping never stopped as Mother stayed so busy doing house work she didn't have time to stay in the living room and give orders.

The four older children had things that they must take care of so the three small children were free to play. I am sure you can understand the problem of three boys sleeping in one small bed and two girls in another small bed in the same room. This was made more complicated because one of our brothers had a kidney problem and our bed would get wet about two o'clock in the morning. This was a horrible experience in the winter time as we would not have any place to go; and with no bathroom or running water in the house we would just have to lay there until morning. We would do a little better in the summer time, as we could get up and go outside and sleep under the stars. However this also had its problems as the bugs and insects were always around to bite and sting, and the morning dew fell on our faces to wake us up. It was a daily chore to drag the wet mattress off the bed and into the yard to dry in the sun, and then bring it back in at bed time. The floor boards in the house were separated so that you could see the ground on a sunny day; and in the winter, the wind blew snow into the house through cracks in the window facing. We thought it was such a blessing when Dad brought home linoleum for our bedroom, as it did cut down on the cold air coming in. I can remember many times sleeping on the floor on a blanket after he covered the floor.

Daddy and us five boys

My Childhood

Ages 9-11

It is so good to look back through the years and be able to remember some of the real good things that filled our lives with precious memories from the age of nine through sixteen. The first event that took place when I was nine years old, Dad worked for the railroad, and we had the privilege of riding the train free. I had an uncle and aunt who lived in Lilly, Louisiana, and they wanted me to come and visit them. Dad got the tickets, and I boarded the train on a hot July morning and headed for Alexander, Louisiana which was the nearest station to Lilly. Uncle Theo was there to meet me.

I well remember what seemed to me a long dusty ride in a pick up truck with no air conditioning, and you dare not roll the window down as you would choke on the dust. We finally made our way back to Lilly and the big plantation that Uncle Theo owned. The plantation had slave huts all around what looked like to me about 200 acres of cotton fields and a company store at the far end.

They had one daughter about 17 years old named Ann Rysinger. Of course that was my uncle and aunt's last name. I couldn't help but think about the song that Tennessee Ernie used to sing. "Saint Peter don't call me 'cause I can't go, I owe my soul to the company store."

This thought came about when I had been there about a week and noticed the conditions under which those poor workers had to live. It made me ashamed to think about complaining about the house where I lived back home, as it looked like a mansion when compared to what the slaves had—just a one room hut without any screens or doors, and some slaves had as many as six children.

Well, we went into the house which was very nice and sat down to a table loaded with everything that could be thought of that was good

A Life of Miracles

to eat. I thought I was in a mansion as they had water in the house and a bathroom at each end.

For the workers, there were two bath houses—one at each end of the cotton field. But it was a good ways to walk to go to the bathroom and take a shower. They were both in the same building that had no windows or doors, and the shower was just a garden hose hanging from a rafter with a cut-off valve and no hot water. How does that make you feel about the place where you live?

Even as a small boy, I said I would never complain about the place where I lived. There were some conditions that took place through the years that called for complaints, but not where we lived. I learned a lot of lessons from that trip, and the greatest lesson wasn't realized until several years later after I had become a Christian and been called to preach.

I recall while preparing a message for a Sunday sermon that my mind went back in time to the visit I had in Lilly. The message was on "Heaven and Why I Want to Go There."

All of a sudden the sight that I saw early one morning as I sat on the porch and watched the slaves come out of the shacks with bags on their backs, moving slowly into the cotton field came back to me. I couldn't help but notice that the ones that I could see did not have on any shoes, or any shirts on their backs, and there arose a sweet humming sound floating ever so softly across the cotton field. All of a sudden as if they had a choir director standing before them they started singing with tenor, alto, soprano, and base voices blending together as they sang the old black spiritual, "When I Get To Heaven."

At that age my hearing was very good, and I could hear the words as if they were sitting on the porch beside me. It brought tears to my eyes then and even now as I try to tell about the experience. Even though I was not a Christian at the time I believe it left a life time memory that will never leave me; and that memory has more meaning now than it did at the time I heard it. The words came so clear as they began to sing, "I got a robe, you got a robe, all God's children got a robe. When we get to heaven, we gonna put on our robe and gonna walk all over God's heaven. When we get to heaven, we gonna put on our robe and gonna walk all over God's heaven. I got shoes, you got shoes, all God's children got shoes. When we get to heaven, we gonna put on our shoes and gonna walk all over God's heaven." My what a lasting experience that has blessed my life in so many different ways.

I also noticed that most of the older workers walked bent over even when not picking the cotton as they had bent over so much from day light to dark for so many years it had left them in this shape. Well. they would then come in at dusk, dragging their pick for the day to have it weighed. Their money would go to the company store as there was seldom any left after their bill was paid except maybe a few nickels. I do hope in reading this portion of my story, that it will make you more thankful for your many blessings.

Well I arrived safely back home but had many other experiences in Lilly that I will always remember. I look forward to one day seeing and hearing those black slaves that have been set free by the wonderful grace of our loving Lord walking the golden streets of heaven and singing. Maybe then they will sing the new song given to them by our heavenly Father.

There is one other event that took place while I was there that also left me with a lesson never learned before. One morning Uncle Theo gave me a sack and told me to go pick cotton, I told him that I didn't know how. He said, "Come on. I will show you how."

Well, I lasted about one hour, and I could not pick any more cotton in that hot July sun. He took the bag soaked it in water, weighed it, and gave me fifty cents. He said, "Now that is top wages."

The real payment came in the lesson that I had learned to never be a cotton picking cotton picker. That night after eating supper the family all gathered around to hear about my trip to Lilly. It was a fun time as they all had some questions to ask about everything. They wanted to know about the train trip; the trip in the truck from Alexander to Lilly; how big the house was; did they have a bathroom and running water inside; and on and on until I got sleepy and said," I am tired and need to go to bed. I will tell you more tomorrow."

I can truthfully say that it was an experience that taught a little nine year old boy a lot of lessons about life that he would have never known, and helped me to look at life in a different way. I guess the greatest lesson was to be more thankful for the good things in life. I just wish that all my brothers and sisters could have been with me for the train

A Life of Miracles

trip because it was very fearful for me. I did not know anyone on the train except the man who took my ticket, and he did talk to me for just a little bit.

Well get a glass of good cold tea, pick up the script, lean back in a comfortable chair, and open up the next page and follow me down the road of my life story. The next portion will come when I was a little older—events that started at about twelve years of age.

My Childhood

Ages 12-15

Most of the events in my childhood taught me lessons that paid off one way are another in later life. In fact I believe they taught me more about life and how to live a better life than most of the lessons that I studied in school.

When I was about twelve years old my grandfather Alexander Morgan, who lived with us at the time, liked to take me fishing. On one occasion, on a very hot day in August he decided to take me to old Nonconnah Creek about one mile from where we lived. We walked all the way and stopped for just a short time to pull up some weeds that had little worms in them that we could use for bait. I guess it was the trips that we took fishing, along with the many trips that I took with my Dad that put the fire burning inside of me to go as often as I could, and the fire has never gone out. But this trip with Granddaddy Morgan almost put out the flame.

While we were sitting on the creek bank waiting for the fish to take our worms in 90 degree weather without any water to drink—and sure would never think of taking a drink of that muddy creek water—Grandad pulled out some chewing tobacco and cut off a piece and began to smack his lips right in my ear. I looked up at him with my eyes all rolled back in my head like a cow that was about to die. He looked down and said, "Hiram, would you like to have a chew?"

I couldn't say "yes sir" fast enough. That was something I wish I had never said, for I put that stuff in my mouth, smacked down on that big chunk of Brown Mule, got choked, and swallowed the whole thing. I turned green as a grass snake and thought I would die before we could get back to the house. He had to carry me most of the way. When we finally arrived, Mother met us at the door and almost fainted when she saw how sick I was. She got a cold rag, put it on my head, gave me a glass of water, turned to her Dad, and ask him what happened. When he told her, which he should never have done, she started giving him a lecture I thought would never end. I finally up-chucked and went to sleep. But you guessed it. I have never put another piece of Brown Mule or any other kind of chewing tobacco in my mouth, and I vowed that day I never would. A lesson I hope you never have to learn. Just take it from me. It was not easy.

~~~~~~~~

I had another experience with my Grandad that taught me another important lesson about life. Grandad was a turn-key at the county jail in Memphis, Tennessee. He took me with him one night to spend the night with him. He had a small apartment with a kitchen, one bed room, and a couch which was all open to the cells where people were locked in. Most of the prisoners were there for drunk driving or family problems, but those in two cells were bad looking. It scared me just to look at them. There was one empty cell in between the other two cells that soon became occupied. Grandad had to go down to the store just a few blocks from the jail, and he told me to stay there and watch the men, but not to open the cell no matter what they would say. Well, I knew I had to find something to do to keep from looking at those two ugly faces, so I found a jar of peanut butter, got a spoon from the kitchen, and sat there and ate almost all of it before Grandad returned. When he came in and saw the almost empty jar, he asked me what happened, and I told him I was hungry and I ate almost the whole jar. He said, "You did not ask me if you could have that to eat." I said, "No sir you were not here." He said, "You are just trying to be smart with me, and you are going to spend the night in that empty cell for stealing that peanut butter." That scared me so much that I began to cry, but tears did not change his mind. Into the cell I went. Well he was merciful. After about two hours of horror, he let me come out and gave me something to eat. I then crawled upon the couch and went to sleep. But I said to myself that I would never steal again, so another good lesson. I don't know of anything that I have taken from anyone that didn't belong to me. And for sure I have never stolen any peanut-butter but still eat some most every day. I guess it might be a temptation if I came to the time when I could not afford to buy some.

I just have to say thanks to dear old Grandad for the good lessons he taught me while he lived. I learned a lot more about life from him, and some things that I learned were through some of the poetry that he wrote. I have copies of many of his poems and have read them many times. It has also inspired me to do some writing of poetry. I will tell about that later on.

,,*,*,*,*,*,*,*

You had better take a big sip of that cold glass of tea and relax in that big soft armchair, for this next event might make you move out to the end of your chair as you try to keep breathing.

It all took place in 1935 when the muddy Mississippi River froze over, and five of us neighborhood boys decided to walk the five miles to see if we could walk across the frozen river.

James Edward Barnes was the oldest in the group, and he had told us that we would need to stay in a straight line. Charles Jr. would lead the way; James would be behind him; Abe Simon would be next in line; Billy Randall would be the next in line; and I would bring up the rear being the youngest. We all wondered why all this was necessary, but it didn't take long to find out.

We arrived at the river and started down the snow and ice covered rocks. I looked up, and there seemed to be a hundred people on the bank looking at the frozen river. We finally made it to the river, lined up, and started making our way toward the other side. We were about half way across when Charles made his next step, and the ice broke open. Charles plunged down into the frozen water.

James caught his arm and told us to lie down on the ice, grab the person's foot in front of us. When he said, "Pull," everyone was to hold tight and scoot backwards. After several minutes that seemed like hours, we finally pulled Charles back on top of the ice. We then went back to the bank, and each of us took off some of our clothing, took Charles' wet clothes off, and built a fire out of drift wood and broken limbs.

We took some sticks that we found on the bank that had forks in them, and made a rack to hang the wet clothes on; and we all gathered around the fire until the clothes were dry. Charles gave us back our garments and put his back on. We then started back home.

One thing I could never understand is that not one person attempted to come down to help us. I know it would have been dangerous for some of them to have tried to make it down that long snow and ice covered rock bank, but it looks like somebody would have at least tried. Anyway, I will always remember why James told us how to start our trip across the water.

Well if you have started breathing normally again, get up and stretch, take another sip of that cold tea, and follow on to the next event.

~~~~~~~~

After that very frightening experience we all returned home, and no one got sick. I guess that was because we were all use to being cold since we never had enough warm clothes to wear in the winter, and I guess our hides just got tough.

We are back at our regular activities: milking the cow; cutting wood for the cook stove; feeding the chickens; slopping the hog; pumping water for washing clothes in the old black pot; and going to the spring to get some good, cold, clean water to drink. We would take two gallon buckets, and try to be careful not to spill any on the way home.

We had to make this half mile trip one way every day, and on Saturday we would make about six trips, as the pump water was so full of iron rust you would turn orange if you took a bath in it. Saturday was always bath night. We all took our turn in the number three wash tub. Mother would bathe the three small children first: Robert, Jack, and Jimmy. Then the two girls, Frances and Laverne, would take theirs next. The water would begin to get a little dark by the time Charles Jr. and myself would have our turn; and when we finished, it was almost muddy looking.

We used some of that homemade lye soap that was made from the grease from the hog that we had just processed in the back yard back in the winter. I don't remember all that Mother used, but I do remember she scooped up ashes from the fire under the big black pot and used them. One thing I do remember was the power in that soap to cut dirt from the body, and it would leave a kind of warm feeling on your body for a good while.

One of the great blessings came when Dad came home from work with one of the big trucks from the railroad loaded with box car doors that were about 10 feet tall and eight feet wide. From the doors he erected a wash house that was about 10 feet by 10 feet and eight feet high. He bought Mother a Maytag washing machine, ran electric line to the wash house and plugged it up. What a wonderful invention. But that was not all. He put a flat top on the building so he could place a 55 gallon drum on top. He drilled a hole in the top, connected a one inch pipe about four feet long to the bottom of the drum, and put a faucet on the bottom of the pipe with a cut off nob. We would get water from the neighbor's well, fill the drum, let the sun heat the water, and boy for the first time in our lives we could take a good warm bath all summer long. But we would be very careful about the amount of water we would use as it was not to easy to carry the water and put it in the drum.

Dad made a ladder to climb to the top, and one would get on the top, tie a rope to the bucket handle where it could be lifted up. We thought all of this took some real love from our Dad. We were all so thankful.

Not long after dad finished the bath house, he put Mother's washing machine with the hand operated close ringer inside, and hooked it up. We would all have fun turning the handle and watching the water run out of the clothes. We thought that was real neat. It sure changed things on wash day at the LeMay house. No more filling up the big black pot with water and building a fire under the pot to heat the water. We didn't have to cut as much wood either. We would just heat a bucket of water on the cook stove in the kitchen, take it out to the wash house, and pour it in that amazing machine. Mother didn't have to do all that hard work of rubbing the clothes on the old rub board and ringing them out by hand. After she was through with the washing we would all go out to the solar dryer, help hang the clothes on the clothes line stretched across the back yard, and say a prayer for the sun to keep shining. No more filling the number three wash tub for our Saturday night bath, as we could all take our turns under that wonderful shower.

Dad had one more modern invention to make life better at our house. He extended our out house, better known as our privy or toilet, from a one holer to a three holer and put a half petition between hole number two and number three. Number three was for the girls, and numbers one and two were for the boys as there were six males and three females that had daily access. There was a box in the corner that was full of newspaper to use instead of a roll hanging from a rack on the wall. I will let you guess what it was used for. One thing is for sure—it was much better than corn cobs; and I am almost sure that most of you have never heard of using corn cobs for this purpose. But I can assure you it was pretty rough.

It was not very long until times got a little better, and we were able to put two racks on the wall; one in number three and one in between numbers one and two. That was a real improvement. I think it really saved money, as we did not have to spend as much on soothing salve. You can imagine how happy we were to enjoy all these new improvements. Even though we have come a long way, we pray that we don't have to return to the "good old days." I am sure we learned to appreciate things more, but we also learned that we could get by on a lot less if we have to. Something our children did not have the blessing of learning.

~ ~ ~ ~ ~ ~ ~ ~

Our house was located in the ideal place for kids to meet and play, as we had a large vacant field right next to our house. There was a big chestnut tree where we would gather out of the hot sun, draw a big circle, and play marbles. That was always one of my favorite games, as I usually ended up with a tobacco sack full of marbles. But sometimes I would lose back. We never did think of that as gambling, because we would always be willing to give the marbles back to the losers so they would have some to lose back next time.

There were several other activities that took place out in the big field. One of the games would include the girls and the boys. We would choose up sides and play ball. We used an old home made ball that would only last for one game and sometimes have to be repaired before the game could be finished. It was made by wrapping string around a rubber ball and covering that with black tape. Our bat would be made from a two inch hickory limb about three feet long.

There were plenty of hickory trees nearby in the woods at the lower end of the big field. It was in these woods that we spent a lot of time. Dad had made us a wagon from some old wheels he picked up at a dump and some boards that he also picked up at different places. There was a long sloping hill in the woods that ran down beside a winding creek that had a tree stump on the edge of the bank where the creek made a big turn at the bottom of the hill. We would see who could come the closest to the stump without turning over into the creek. Needless to say we all had our turn of getting a good mud bath as we would flip over into the muddy water. I am glad it was never water enough to cover your head—only about two feet deep.

There were also grape vines hanging from the tall trees that offered a lot of fun. They would swing high over a ditch below, and several times we would have to go home and get patched up from a fall. Just lucky enough, no one was ever hurt real bad—just maybe enough to bring a tear or two. Well it was all worth the bumps an bruises, as back then we had no TV to watch, bicycles to ride, or at that age no cars to ride in; and it was too far to walk and cost too much to attend a movie theater.

Not very far down old highway 51 toward Whiteheaven High School is where I received my early education. Not all of it was from the printed page, but I believe most of it was learned through experiences that happened daily. After walking about one mile in the blistering July sun, you would come to the old Nonconnah Creek. This is a an Indian name meaning, "NO FISH." I can testify that whoever named the creek knew what they were doing, as I spent many hours bobbing a worm up and down in the deepest hole I could find. I cannot remember ever catching many fish, but I have caught several crawfish.

The experiences that we had in the muddy water was mostly from jumping off of a tree limb into about four feet of water and splashing around. When a big rain would come we would all head out to the creek to ride logs down the creek as the water was very swift and high.

On one of our trips to the fast running stream Harold Craig, one of our group of five boys ages 12-15, was going to lead us in our ride on this trip that would lead us to the Mississippi River. We had only gone about a half mile when Harold was snatched into the water by a low tree limb hanging just one foot above the rising water. This was the end of our ride for the day, as we all fell off our logs to help find Harold and pull him out of the danger of drowning as he had hurt his arm and could not swim. We were very lucky as the water was not over four feet deep and real narrow at this point but was on the rise, and that made it very hard to stand up. But lucky enough we were able to pull him out before the water washed him down stream. We had to get out and take him home as he was hurting real bad. We all took times carrying him on our back or two would make what we called a pack saddle, and he would sit on their arms, and they would carry him walking sideways which was very difficult.

I cannot remember ever riding logs down the creek after that frightening experience. On another occasion when the water was high from rain, we went to swim, and some black boys had ridden their bikes down from the city about five miles away. One of the boys jumped in and was swept under a log and got hung and could not get loose. The black boys ran away screaming, but we jumped in and tried to get him out. The water was so swift we were not able to get him out in time, and he drowned. One of the blacks that left had called for a fire truck to come for help. They came but too late.

Well I guess by now that many of you younger folks that are taking the time to wade through the woods with us are wishing you could have lived back in the good old days. For the most part the wooded areas where we had so much fun have all been removed and riding in our home-made wagon, swinging from the grape vines, climbing up a young sapling, and riding it down to the ground can no longer be enjoyed. The trees have been cut down and used for building material, and the ditches have been filled in by the big bulldozers. There are no more grape vines swinging from trees, and the dirt paths that we used to walk have been turned into concrete or black top. The hillsides are now all covered with houses or condos, and the surrounding area filled up with places of business. Everything seems to be changing very fast.

My Childhood

Ages 15-16

I have now reached the age of fifteen, and many of the activities that occupied my mind and time have turned the corner and headed in another direction. I have become more interested in music and girls, and no longer care about getting down on my knees to shoot marbles, ride down the hill in a wagon, or swing across a deep ditch on a grape vine. I no longer care to sit on the bank of old Nonconnah Creek and drown worms. Now I enjoy a trip with Dad to Sardis Lake, or Tunica Lake in Mississippi where we can catch a cooler full of big crappie or bream, come back home, and have a big fish fry. It was at this point in time where even that was pushed aside for my activities in music that led to my getting to know girls my age.

Dad would have his friends come to our house on weekends to play music, and I would always enjoy watching and listening. It was not long before I could pick up the guitar and play along. We always had music in the fall of the year when the crops began to be harvested. We would sit on the front porch with big buckets of black eyed peas to shell or a basket of corn to be shucked and listen to Dad sing some of the old heartwarming songs called ballads. I can remember him singing a song that would bring tears to my eyes even as it does now just thinking about how much I would love to hear him once more. The line in the song that would always touch my heart was, "If I could recall all the heart aches, dear old Daddy, I've caused you to bear, if I could erase those lines from your face and bring back the gold to your hair. If God would but grant me the power, just to turn back the pages of time, I'd give all if I could atone to that silver-haired Daddy of mine.

My Musical Experiences

My first experience with trying to play the guitar came about when I was very young, about nine years of age. Dad and and my older brother were the only two in our family that could play music, and they were both sick with the flu. Dad told me to get the guitar and sit next to the bed, and he would show me where to put my fingers in order to make a chord. He taught me the C, D, and G Cords. I sat there and played them over and over until I could finally play a very simple song that only used two Cords: C and G. I sat there and played the song for over an hour. "Roses love sunshine. Violets love dew. Angels in heaven know I love you."

I believe that my singing and playing helped Dad and my brother to get better, as they were much better the next day and were able to get up out of bed. It could have been that they thought the family needed to hear some better music.

I do remember though my Mother acting so proud of me for learning the three cords so quickly. I guess it was because she spent so much time going over my spelling lessons, and it didn't seem to help one bit. I still have trouble with spelling. But thanks to the good Lord, my playing instruments got better as time went on. I took up playing in the school band and learned to play the clarinet, drums, and sax. I am not a finished musician but have had a lot of enjoyment in playing several instruments for my own pleasure. I now enjoy picking Dad's old Martin mandolin, blowing on a french harp, playing a piano, or organ.

It was at the age of 15 that five of my friends and my brother Charles started a cowboy band. Frank Davis played lead guitar; his sister Olive played accordion; Charles Starks played steel guitar; and Shorty Comer played base fiddle. My brother played back up guitar, and I played clarinet and did the singing. We played for schools, some night clubs, and a lot of civic clubs around Memphis.

I could never forget an invitation we had from a friend of ours to go to his home town to play for a community dance. His name was Dick Gaffard, and he was from Slayden, Tennessee way back in the boon docks. We left home about six o'clock on Saturday afternoon with eight people, and all the instruments in a van driven by Frank Davis. We had three tires to blowout before we finally arrived about two o'clock in the morning. But the people were still there waiting on us, and we played music until daylight on Sunday morning. That was some kind of an experience.

There were many other things that happened in that horrible experience to and from Slayden, Tennessee. We were passing through Summerville at about midnight. Dad and his friend Elmer Clark were in our group, and they were going along to put on a black face act.

Missouri Pacific Minstrel Show Black Face Act

They had both been drinking and were getting pretty drunk and said they needed to make a pit stop. Frank pulled over to the curb to let them out, but we could not see anything open. They took off down the street and came back in a few minutes bringing a country ham. We asked them where they got the ham. They said it was hanging on a rack out in front of a store. We managed to find the store, and put it back before we proceeded on our journey.

They gave us a lot of trouble on the trip going but slept almost all the way back home. That was a good relief. Well we finally pulled into Memphis about noon on Sunday morning, and we were taken to our

A Life of Miracles

homes where we all went straight to bed. At least I know that Dad, Charles, and I all went to bed and slept until Monday morning.

We had not been home but a few days when Frank came to the house and told us that we were invited to play on the Speed Base radio program next Saturday. Speed Base owned a Music Store in Memphis and had a regular Saturday radio program. We did go and Speed invited us to join his orchestra and play with them every Saturday. He ask me to be the soloist for the program.

Speed Base radio program

We had been on for about three weeks, and I received a letter from a man in New York that wanted me to come to New York for an all-expense-paid trip to have an interview. Mother said I could not do that and answered his letter letting him know that I would not be coming.

I am sure that was the best thing that could have happened, even though I really wanted to go. I did not know at that time what God had planned for my life, but looking back I am sure the best thing took place. If I had accepted his request it could have meant a different direction for my life than I would have wanted for I did have a good singing voice at that time.

We continued playing with Speed and other engagements for another year, and then we began to break up and find other interests. It was a very short time after we stopped playing on the radio, that we had our last civic club invitation. This was the very beginning of the real romance in my life.

Beginning of My Romance

I have now come to the age of sixteen, and the real romance in my life has started. There were very few times in my life up to this time when I really had any experiences with romance. I would sit on the school bus and talk with different girls at times but never went anywhere with any of them. Mother talked me into going to the fair with one of our community girls that was more like a sister to me, but mother was told that she had a crush on me. That was not a very good experience.

Our bus driver's daughter asked me to come to her house for Easter dinner. I remember going and walking through the snow about one mile to where she lived. I had a good dinner and was treated very nice, but I just did not feel that I would ask her for a date, even though she let me know that she would go if asked. I did not ever ask, but we did sit together on the bus at times.

The only other time that I ever went out with another girl, I was asked by a friend of mine who was much older than I, if I would go with his girl friend's sister on a blind date to a dance where Benny Goodman would be playing. I told him you know that I don't have the money to go to Rainbow Lake Club, and he said he would take care of the tickets, so I went. That was not a very good experience. When I got back home I had to soak my feet, as she had stepped all over them, and my toes were black and blue.

Now for the real thing.

~~~~~~~~

We were playing for the civic club in our community, and I looked up and saw this beautiful girl coming in with a friend of mine. My heart almost jumped out of my shirt. When I had a break I asked him who she was. "Her name is Nancy Craig. I was asked by a friend to go with her on a blind date." "Are you interested in her?" I asked. "Not at all," he said.

"Could I meet her and see if I could take her home?" He said, "I wish you would."

Well I did, and she said it would be all right with her. We had a thirty minute break coming up, and I ran all the way home, ran into the house, changed into the best clothes that I had, and told mother that I had fallen in love.

"You don't even know what love is," she shouted as I ran out the door and back to the club just in time for the last session.

My friend Frank said he would take us to her home. We stopped and had a BBQ and milk shake and then proceeded to 1006 Philadelphia Street. I asked her if I could come back to see her the next week end, and she said yes.

The long trip from the country road in South Memphis to 1006 Philadelphia Street in East Memphis near the fairgrounds was traveled many times in various ways but mostly by walking. I would start back home about nine o'clock, and if I was lucky someone would stop and give me a ride. One night a man picked me up. We had not gone far until he was saying things that I did not want to hear. I could tell from the things that he said that he must be gay, and I was in trouble. I began to think of the way to get out of the car, so I asked him if he liked beer. His reply was quick and loud, "I sure do."

I told him to pull in at Five Gables, a place where we use to play music which was only about one half mile from our house, and I would go in and get some beer for us. I had never had any to drink myself, but my intention was not to buy beer but go out the back door, cut through a wooded area behind the club, and run home as fast as I could. You know what? It worked. I don't know where he went to from there, but I am sure he left mad. Ha Ha.

It is real strange that on another occasion I had a real close call with death, and it took place right in front of Five Gables. A man had picked me up, and we were just riding along talking about good things in life, and a car of drunks pulled out of Five Gables and hit us head on. The driver of our car was knocked out, and my knees were stuck in the dashboard. My head hit the windshield, and it pinched a hunk out of my cheek. I pulled my knees loose, reached up and took my hunk of meat out of the window, and put it in my pocket. I looked out the window and saw bodies scattered all over the road and knew that they had to be pulled out of the road or get hit. I made my way to the first person I could get to and pulled her to the edge, and then I passed out.

The next thing I knew a lady was bending over me with a wet cloth and wiping my face. She ask me where I lived, and she said, "We will take you home. When we got to the door, mother opened the door and fainted when she saw me. Dad was standing behind her and caught her. The people were so nice, they took me to the hospital and waited until they took stitches in my face, and took care of other things, and then brought me back home.

This was a very horrifying experience for me, and caused me to spend three weeks with my leg elevated and taking pain pills twice a day. I had to keep ice packs on my knees for two weeks, and that was not any fun. One thing that was real good about my recovery was the attention I got from Mother and also my brothers and sisters. They all wanted to sit near the couch and ask me about all the details of the accident. The man that was driving the car that I was in came almost every day to see how I was doing and would always bring me some kind of gift, and ask if there was anything that I wanted. I thought that was so nice of him. After about three weeks I was able to stand up and walk some but still very sore. We had to go to court and give an account of what happened as we saw it. The man that was driving the car that hit us took the car without permission from his brother's yard—our neighbor.

There were six people in the car, three boys and three girls, and they were all taken to the hospital but were all released with minor problems. Some of them still had patches on their faces from the wreck. That was my first experience to be in a court room, and I was ill at ease to say the least and glad when it was all over. The man driving the stolen car was fined and had to spend some time in jail. Well that was just another experience that came about when I was dating Nancy, my future wife.

~~~~~~~~

Nancy had a half brother named Jan. He would always come and sit by us on the porch as he knew that was a way to get a nickel so he could buy a cold drink. I would give him the nickel so he would leave us alone. I am not sure how many nickels he received over the two years that we dated, but it was once a week and you can figure that one out for yourself.

One night as we sat on the steps making plans for our wedding date we both fell asleep, and the milk man woke us up when he had to go up the steps to put the milk on the porch. I was so afraid of what would happen when I got home having been out all night, so I went to my uncles house and ask him to take me home. He was so good to me, and I asked him to tell my Dad, his brother; that I had spent the night with him. When I told him what happened he just laughed and said ok. I never told Dad what happened until Nancy and I were married.

Our dating was much different than the average 16 year old today. There were no cars to drive or even bikes to ride so everything had to be in walking distance. On some rare occasions one of my few friends with access to autos would take us to a movie. Nancy and I spent most of our time just sitting on the front porch enjoying each other's company. She lived in walking distance to the fairgrounds, and we would go there when I had a few dollars to spend. We would get something to drink, and a bag of popcorn, and sit on the bench, and watch the other people enjoy riding the merry-go-round, and taking in the other activities.

We dated for almost two years, and Hitler was marching his troops through the Balkans. We knew World War II was not far from taking place, as Hitler made it very plain that he was going to rule the world with his superior race. By 1940 he had already taken over most of the Balkan States with his goose step army.

With the knowledge of what was inevitable for our future we thought we had better get married. This meant that I would have to drop out of school and get ready for the draft. I knew if we got married that I would have to go to work. Well I did, and so did Nancy. I went to work for Mr. Canistrary in the grocery store where we traded. I would put up stock, wait on customers in the store, and deliver groceries to the people that called in their orders. Some of the people lived about 10 miles from the store, almost to the Mississippi state line. Nancy went to work at Woolworth's 5 & 10 cent store, and we began to plan our wedding date.

On October, 31st 1942 a friend of mine, Gerald Biggs, who owned a car, took us to Horn Lake, Mississippi to get married. My

Dad had arranged to have a reception at the Trainman's Hall where he conducted the Minstrel Show for several years. That was quite an experience.

    We went home with Dad and Mom and spent the night with them. They gave us their bedroom and said they would sleep on the couch. I was so sleepy that I fell off to sleep, and when I woke up they had put a teddy bear in my arms, and Nancy was gone. They had left and taken her to a movie.

Our Married Life

The first three months of our married life, we lived with Nancy's mother on Philadelphia Street. A friend of mine, Jim Gipson, built us a one room house on the back of his property. There was no running water, no bathroom, but we were next door to Dad's and Mom's house, so we used their outdoor privy; and we were able to get our water from Mr. Gipson's well. We bought a bucket for the water, and it sat on a stand by the door.

We had a lot of fun trying to measure everything that we bought to make sure it would fit in that one small room. We went to Sears, and bought a couch that made into a bed and a small gate leg table that had folded sides. We still have that table and use it sometimes when we have company with children. It is like me, a little wobbly, but can still hold two plates, a knife and fork. Now it spends most of the time holding up a flower arrangement. We also bought two chairs, which have been gone a long time.

Nancy and her Mother both worked at Woolworth's 5&10 in downtown Memphis. Several of us guys had a car pool, and we would take Nancy to her Mother's house when it was time to go to work. She and her Mother would ride the street car to work and back. We would pick her up at her Mother's on our way home from work. This lasted only five months, because World War II began. I received my papers to report for duty on February 14, 1943. Nancy moved back in with her Mother, and Jim Gipson said the house would be waiting for us when I returned from duty.

I served two years, nine months, 14 days, six hours and 15 minutes. I shouted, "Hallelujah" when I received my Honorable Discharge, and I headed for HOME!

We were able to move in with my parents when I returned. Four of my siblings had married and moved out. We stayed with my parents until we found our first home to purchase. It was on the corner of

Watson and New Willow in Memphis, Tennessee. We paid the big price of $2,500. It was a two bedroom, one bath home. Everything was small.

A man named Dawkins, built homes for the returning soldiers. He wanted to help us out and get us in affordable housing.

Nancy and me

My Army Experience

Age 18

I'm in the Army now

Leaving home was a very sad experience not only for me, but for all the others that were on that troop train headed for Fort Oglethorpe, Georgia. It was a day that I will never forget as that train pulled out of the station, and I waved goodby to my wife and mother standing there waving with tears running down their cheeks. I could hardly see them, for I also, along with all the others on that troop train, was wiping the tears from my eyes. I think all of us must have been thinking, "Will this be the last time I will ever see my loved ones?"

Looking back to the end of the war there were some who never had the privilege of returning home alive. That was and still is very sad. I never pass a Military Cemetery, but what I don't have lumps come up in my throat. We had not gone very far until the train had to stop and one man had to be taken off and be taken to the hospital. I never heard what happened to him, but he did not show up at Oglethorpe, Georgia.

It was a very hot day in July when we pulled into the Station in Georgia early in that afternoon. We were greeted by a Staff Sergeant who marched us to a truck that carried us to Fort Oglethorpe and led us to a building where we received a sack lunch and a soft drink of water. After a short period of time we were led to a room where we received a lecture for about one hour about the Army Rules, and what would happen to us if those rules were not followed. We then had to go have our hair all cut off and receive several shots. We were lined up and marched to a barracks where we spent the night. The next morning we were up at six o'clock, ate breakfast, and then were called one at a time to receive our assignment of the branch of service that we were to serve in.

Our appointment would be to the Infantry, Air Force, or Field Artillery. We had to have a physical prior to our assignment and take the report with us. When I was called in, I was told that I could return home if I chose to. My physical report stated that I had 3rd degree flat feet.to flat for the requirements ahead of me. I chose to stay. I wanted to do my part in serving our country and helping to protect our people. I was then assigned to Fort Bragg, North Carolina to the 155th Field Artillery Battalion as Private First Class. Several of us were loaded in an Army truck and taken to Fort Bragg. They had a good lunch prepared for us hungry guys when we arrived.

We were greeted by the First Sergeant who looked like a pit bull dog. He was a full time Army man, rough as a cob. He lined us up and marched us to the mess hall. After we finished our lunch we were marched to a conference room where we received another lecture about Army Policy at Fort Bragg. We were then assigned to our barracks and bed number. We were dismissed and told to go to the supply room and pick up our equipment. It was a footlocker that was to be placed at the foot of the bunk or bed and sheets and blanket that was to be put on the bunk with perfection.

We received a barracks bag full of other items: canteen, leggings, socks, shoes, daily rations for use when on maneuvers or field trips. We also received an M 1 rifle with ammunition, our daily clothes, and our dress uniform. It was a real load to be carried to the barracks. Most everyone had to go back several times to exchange items that did not fit. My shoes were so big that I could put them on, do an about face, and the shoes would still be pointed in the same direction.

My dress coat was large enough to fit a 300 pound man, and I was just 155 pounds soaking wet. Well, after getting all the equipment changed, the bunk made up, and our shoes polished to a glossy shine, it was now time for inspection. In came the old bull dog—Sergeant Tazalosky. With a name like that you can just imagine what he looked like, and he talked just as bad as he looked. We had to stand at the foot of our bunk at attention. When he came to each bunk, he would look us up and down, inspect the bunk, and if not perfect he would throw the sheets back and demand it be made up again.

We had to do KP duty if it was not right the second time. That meant peeling potatoes, washing dishes, and mopping the floor of the mess hall. After inspection inside, we would go out in front of the barracks with our rifles, line up, and stand at attention for rifle inspection. It had better be clean or more KP. By the time all this was over it was time for a one hour break before our evening meal. Then we would go to the conference room for our instructions for the next day. We were told to be in front of the barracks at six o'clock sharp with polished boots ready to march to the mess hall for breakfast.

Every day started at six o'clock in the morning and ended at nine o'clock in the evening with different activities each day and lights out at 10 o'clock. There was never too much action by anyone after lights out as everyone was tired from the activities of the day. We would go on field trips and walk about twenty miles in the boiling hot North Carolina sun. After we had only gone ten miles I dropped to the back of the formation so that I could slip out of line and fill my canteen if we happen to pass a stream of water. We finally came near a cow pond, and I went over and dipped up a canteen full of water. We were warned about doing this as it could make us sick. I had to choose the risk as I was so thirsty. I was very lucky because I did not get caught getting the water, and I never got sick. I drank the whole thing.

That evening when we returned to the base we were given free time to shower and prepare for the evening meal. Some days we would attend classes to study about different guns, and booby traps. The big guns were 155 millimeter howitzers. There were also classes on small arms and demolitions. There were times when we would have to go through obstacle courses, some during the day and some at night, climb high walls, crawl under barbed wire with machine gun fire going over our heads with tracer bullets, and explosives going off all around us. This was very dangerous. One boy was killed as he raised up and was hit by a tracer bullet. That was a real sad time for all of us.

I had been promoted to rank of Corporal. My duty was to shoot the machine guns, sometimes at night, and that was a scary time for me as I was afraid that someone might get scared, raise up, and get hit. I was glad when each event was over and no one was hurt. We went out to the grenade range one day to practice the use of grenades. I was in charge of ten boys.

One of our team pulled the pin and threw the grenade early. I rushed out and picked it up and threw it as far as I could. We were lucky that no one was injured. The young man's name was Gilento and was finally given a dishonorable discharge from the service as he had done so many things that endangered the lives of so many men. It wasn't long after this experience that I was promoted to Drill Sergeant and was put in charge of our platoon of 63 men.

My Army Experience

Age 19

One of my many jobs was to get the men out for inspection every morning and march them to the mess hall for breakfast. It was my job to inspect every bunk to make sure they would pass the Bull Dog's inspection when he came through. He would come through some time when we were out on field trips or out on the Howitzer range where it was my job as section Chief to see that the piece was in proper place and ready for action. When we came back in, we could tell that he had been there as somebody would have to remake their bunk with a note on the bunk to report for KP after the evening meal.

The Howitzer that we were using had a crew of five men, and we had a battery of four guns. I was the one in charge and gave the orders to fire. My orders came down from the CP where the Lieutenant in charge would send the amount of powder charge to use, as the amount of powder would determine the distance the ninety pound projectile would travel. A number 11 charge would send the ninety pound projectile twenty miles. It was equipped with a nose cone that would explode when the projectile hit the target. I believe it was here that my hearing loss began. When I would give the command to fire, I would be standing at the right side of the number one gun and would get the blast from all four guns. Many times I would go in with my nose bleeding and ears hurting so bad I couldn't go to sleep. They did not give me any ear plugs to use. This was my job until my last year as Gunner Chief. I taught small arms and demolitions for a little while and then was raised to Staff Sergeant and put in charge of the motor pool and work shop. I remained there until the war was ended, and I received my discharge in 1946.

It was very hard for me to accept being left behind when my training cycle ended, and all my friends were shipped out but me. I was told by our commanding officer that I was needed to stay in the camp and be there to help train the next group. It was after this took place that Nancy came to be with me, and I had rented an apartment in town. Nancy got a job in a grocery store, and it was not long until she brought forth our first child, Nan Marie. We called her our little Tar Heel. I was present at the time of the birth, and they insisted that I watch the delivery. I lasted about five minutes, and I passed out. The Army nurse said this was the first time they had ever lost a father and got a big laugh out of my weakness.

My Army Days Come To An End

Ages 20-22

I was given an offer by our Commanding Officer to stay in the Army, be sent to officers training school for one year, and come out as a 1st Lieutenant, but I was ready to head back to Tennessee with my wife and new born baby. About halfway back home I was wishing that I had taken the offer to stay in service, as the trip was getting to me.

Nan could do nothing but cry, I had trouble with my ears hurting so bad that I had to stop and have them give me pain shots, and medication to help me get home. We had to stop at a motel just before heading across the Smokey Mountains. Nan still could not sleep, and we stayed there about two hours, got up and started on our way again.

I was driving a 1935 Buick that I bought before leaving Fort Bragg. It had mechanical brakes, and we were headed for ice covered roads in the mountains. I was really wishing that I had not bought the car and would have purchased train tickets. But that was too late. When we started up the mountain cars were off the road on every side, but we kept going. It was one of the worst driving experiences that I have ever had. I believe the mechanical brakes were our life saver as they would not stop real fast and make the car slide off the road.

We finally made it to the other side about daylight. Boy did that sun look good. We were able to make it on home about eight o'clock that evening. I will never forget Mother meeting us at the door and asking what happened. She said she had been up all night praying for us as she felt we were in trouble. We had written Mother and told her what time we thought we would be home. Of course we were delayed because of the stop for treatment and slow travel through the mountains. Like the words of the song said, "My it's good to be back home again."

We pick up now from the time that we got married and moved into our first home on Watson and New Willow in east Memphis. It was after we returned home from service that we stayed with Mom and Dad until we were able to move into our home. I went to work at Anderson Clayton Cotton Company for a short time then to the Bluff City Buick Company where I worked until my move to Nashville, Tennessee to work for Nashville Motors. I will have more to say about that experience a little later when I come to the part about the reason for my move to Nashville in 1948. It seems to me that from this time on it was a life of miracles.

My Musical Experiences

Age 25-65

I have always had a love for music, and my favorites are gospel and country. It was always a real joy for me to be able to rare back in my easy chair with a good cold glass of sweet milk and a bowl full of graham crackers after a hard days work and listen to gospel or country music until the milk and crackers were gone and my eyes were too heavy to stay open.

The Blackwood Brothers, the Gaithers, the Speer family, Tennessee Ernie Ford, and many others would give me a real spiritual lift and get me ready for a good night's sleep. When I came to that time in my life when I was able to buy a car with a radio, it was a refreshing experience to turn on the radio and listen to the music that thrilled my heart as I would drive back and forth to work. I am sure if they had CD players and ear phones back then, I would have been seen walking the streets doing my daily visitation to the sick and lost people in our church field with ear phones on my head. Of course I would have taken them off before I knocked on their door.

I had learned the words to many good gospel songs and began to sing them in churches. Sometimes when I preached and one of the songs fit into the message, I would just rare back and begin to sing. I believe that many of the revival meetings that I was asked to preach came about because the pastor who invited me knew that I would sing as well as preach. What always amazed me was that many of them would ask me to come back several times. This all led to one of the real thrills in my musical experiences.

One of the ladies in the church where I was pastor; ask me why I had not had a tape made of some of the songs that I would sing from time to time. Really, I had never even thought about that. But I did make it a matter of prayer.

After a few months I received an answer to my prayers. We were having a revival at Rugby Hills Baptist Church where I was pastor. We contacted Jack Marshall, piano player for the Blackwood Brothers Quartet, and asked him if he could come and play for our revival. I was really surprised that he would have the time as the Blackwood Brothers were in demand in those days; but we lucked up, and he came.

He was a real blessing to our church. I asked him while he was there if he could play the piano for me to cut a tape, and again I was really excited as he said that he would and would call me the next time he was recording in the studio down town in Memphis. I was so up-beat that I called Mrs. Stiltz at Una and told her that progress was being made on cutting the album, and that Jack Marshall would be playing the piano for me. She is the lady who had asked early on if I had ever recorded the songs that I would sing from time to time. She seemed to be real excited and told me to just let her know how much she needed to send me.

I got busy getting the songs together and finding out how many were free domain. That means they could be recorded without charge. When all the research was finished there was only two songs that required royalty to be paid to the song writer, and the total cost for everything was $ 360.00. I was so happy that when I found out the price I wanted to shout. I had just finished a revival and received enough to make the payment myself. Well God seemed to be really blessing me, as Jack called and told me to meet him the next Monday night at WREC Radio Station, where there was a studio for recording. I was in a revival that started on that Monday night, but he told me to meet him at 9:30, so I felt I could make it. When I finished the message that night I was soaking wet, but did not have time to go by the house to change clothes. So I just went straight to the radio station, and there we stayed until 11:30. We got the album cut and ready for the 300 recordings to be made and put into album covers. The covers had my picture on the front and "Salvation Songs" on the cover.

Yes, I did call the nice lady and let her know about everything and told her I would send her an album. When I received the albums, two hundred were sold, and enough money came from the sales that more than paid for the cost. There are still several copies of the album floating around today. I gave several away.

Recording Love Songs with my brother Jimmy

My Musical Experiences

Age 65-87

My singing came to an end at about the age of sixty five as old mother nature finally took her toll. Sixty-three years in the full time ministry, preaching three times a week, and holding ten day revival services on a pretty regular schedule finally wore out my vocal cords. I still try sometimes to sing to myself, but I've just about come to the place where I don't like to hear myself. But I still have enough left to preach now and then.

My hearing has become so bad that it is hard for me to tell when my guitar is in tune, and when I finally get it to where it sounds pretty good to me, I have trouble knowing if I am in one key, and the guitar is in another key. Who cares. I can still lean back in my easy chair, put my head set on, and hear good enough to enjoy one of my tapes. I have just bought some knew hearing aids, and I can hear the church choir for the first time. I can even make out the different voices singing soprano, alto, tenor, and bass, and that is real progress.

Maybe, if I stay around in this old flesh long enough someone will learn how to perform ear transplants. It looks like they could since they are smart enough to transplant just about every other organ in the body including the heart. I am so grateful at my age to be able to hear my wife call me for dinner, and I have good eye sight so I can read the messages on my computer and stay in contact with all my wonderful family and friends. I can still see how to read God's Word, and that is a blessing to me. His word has always been sweet—like sweet music to me. So I will just go on singing in my heart unto the good Lord until He rolls back the curtains of heaven and calls me home. Then when I arrive, I will sing the new song that He will give us to sing in Heaven. But until then, my heart will go on singing.

My Poetry

Ages 45-87

    I have been writing poetry for many years, but most of my poetry has been written in the past fifteen years. I wrote poems about people that meant so much to my life. Many of them I would write and read at their funeral service. Poetry to me has to come from a deep feeling from experiences that I have had in life. Some of my experiences have come through people, and some from nature, and some from deep feelings about our country.

    I enjoyed writing some about events that took place in our family, such as Christmas and other occasions. The greatest poem that I ever wrote was given to me by my blessed Lord. We were having a church youth camp at Standing Stone State Park in 1967. There were about 120 children ages 9-16 and about 10 adults. I would give them a passage in the Bible to read, and tell them to find them a spot alone, and no one was to be with them. I told them to read the Bible verse, have prayer, look around, and listen while God spoke, then to write down what came to them.

    I was amazed at many of the things that were read by the children when we met at ten o'clock for share time. But I was so moved by what God gave to me. I was seated on a log next to a brook that ran into a lake just a few yards down from where I was seated. There were beautiful mountains all around. It was very early in the morning, and there was a heavy fog over the mountain. After I read the passage and had prayer, I looked up and saw the sun pushing the fog away. Just like a flash of a light, the words that started coming to me seemed as if God was just right there speaking to me. Within five minutes the poem was written: "I Saw God This Morning."

    I will have a copy of the poem in this portion of the book along with several others. But something wonderful has happened across the years as I met a friend who was a professional frame maker. He was interested in world hunger like I was and still am; and he agreed to frame the poems for the cost of materials. I have taken them to churches where I have pastored or held revivals, and in the past six years over five thousand dollars has been given to World Hunger. Thanks, Jim Solomon, for your devotion to World Hunger.

There were two other experiences with the poem, "I Saw God This Morning" that I need to mention before moving on. I had received some information from the International Society Of Poetry about a meeting they were having in Washington. Everyone interested could attend and have an opportunity to read their poetry before a group of judges and have a chance to win a prize or recognition of some kind. I thought about the invitation for some time as it was in the month of February, 2001 and very cold. But after some time I thought it would be fun, so we bought our tickets and took off. I never realized how many people would be there, but there were over 2,000 from all over the world.

We were grouped for the reading session with people who had written religious poetry. There were 55 in our group. We were given about five minutes to say a few words about the poem and then read it. I received first place in our group and was awarded a medallion and a certificate of Merit. My poem was put in the International Society of Poetry Book on page 82.

We went to the closing awards meeting, and the man that used to play Bobo the Clown was the MC. A woman from a foreign country went home with the big prize, and I wish you could have been there and heard the poem. It was so worldly, and in some points very vulgar. Well, just goes to show what the thinking of the judges must have been. Like most things we observe today. Just keep it in the gutter, and you will please most of the people.

The other experience really had more meaning for me, as my Brother Jimmy called me and said he would like to put music to the poem. He did and sent me a CD that I thought would go good with the sale of the poem for World Hunger. He sent some copies, and told me that he would supply all that I needed at his cost. Some who have received a copy have been very complimentary. He also sent me a copy of the copy-right that he ordered.

Well before we move along to my hobbies, here are a few of my poems.

I Saw God This Morning

I saw God this morning, just past the break of day,
When the sun came over the mountainside and pushed the fog away.
The birds were singing in the trees, with tones so soft and sweet,
They matched the freshness in the air that makes a day complete.
The little bees that buzzed around in a very cheerful way,
Reminded me of the happiness
That I could know today.
The mighty oak that towered high above the other trees,
Spoke as it stood so straight and tall of the god who stands by me.
The tender touch of the gentle breeze that whispered through the air,
Seemed to speak of God's great love
That is found at a place of prayer.
Yes, I saw God in everything as I sat beside the brook,
And looked at things that He has made
And read His blessed book.

Hiram LeMay

America, My Home

America, that exciting name
Brings a smile to every face.
For in this world in which we live
There is no greater place!
Old Glory still waves her colors
From our Capitol for all to see.
America, the beautiful land,
The home of the brave and the free.
As you travel through this land
From north to south, and east to west,
It doesn't take you long to realize
We are blessed with the very best!
From the majestic snow covered mountains
In the north and in the west,
Where millions go to ski and find A quiet place to rest.
Then we go to the deep, deep south, And walk on the ocean sand;
There feel the tender touch of the ocean breeze,
Bow our head and fall on our knees
Thanking God for America, this wonderful land.

World Peace

World peace is a heart felt desire
Expressed in literature, poetry and song.
Yet, we wonder if we will ever live
To see the world peace for which we long.
It seems when fighting in one place
Is about to come to an end
We see on the news another place
Where the fighting will soon begin.
World peace on planet earth will never come
By wars that claim our young daughters and our sons
I am convinced the older I become,
That world peace is only in God's beloved Son.
One day He will come, His kingdom to restore.
There will be no fighting or wars anymore.
He alone will fight that final battle,
With the anti-Christ and sin.
Then we will experience world peace,
And that peace will never end!

Hiram LeMay

Mother's Prayer

I've heard many mothers say
They would take time at the beginning
of each dawning day
To meet with God their burdens to share
In a special place called "a place of prayer."
For important decisions they knew they must make,
They couldn't afford to make a mistake.
So each and every dawning day
They take their time to stop and pray.
Then at the close of a busy day,
Again, they take the time to pray.
Thanking God for His loving care
And the answers to their every prayer.

A Life of Miracles

Winter in Tennessee

I looked out my window
And gazed all around At the beautiful sight
Of the snow covered ground.
The temperature had dropped
To fourteen degrees,
And icicles were hanging
From the limbs of the trees.
The North Wind was blowing
Across the fresh fallen snow,
Dropping the wind chill
To a chilling zero.
Then the sun came through the clouds.
What a beautiful sight to see.
As the snow started melting from the ground
And the ice began falling from trees.
It all happened so quickly,
It was easy to see,
We were experiencing
A typical winter in Tennessee.

Hiram LeMay

Winter Sports

It's winter time, that's easy to see.
With snow on the ground and in all the trees.
The temperature is ten degrees,
And the wind is blowing with a gusty breeze.
The chill factor is thirty below,
As the Raiders are playing Buffalo.
It is really a sight for the eye to behold
As they slip and slide in the bitter cold.
Both teams are playing with heart and soul,
Trying hard to make it to the Super Bowl.
This one thing we do know . . .
Only one team is going to go!
Right now its hard to tell
Who will represent the N.F.L.
If today, Buffalo can prevail
They could well represent the AFL.
No matter which team happens to play,
It is going to be an exciting day!

The Day After Christmas

Tis the day after Christmas
And all seems to be quiet, But mother's house is a horrible sight.
There is paper and tinsel all over the floor,
And the postman is knocking at our front door.
In his hand are the bills from the spending we have done.
It sure cost a lot for just one day of fun!
The sink is full of dirty dishes and glasses galore;
Of pots and pans and a whole lot more!
All of the children are as ill as they can be,
From eating the goodies found under the tree.
The toys don't run, 'cause the batteries are dead;
And dad can't help for he's still in the bed.
He was up all night, just one night before,
Putting toys together in the middle of the floor.
Some parts wouldn't fit and others weren't there.
He became so disturbed he thought he'd pull out his hair!
Mother is trying to fix up the place, But she has such a tired look on her face.
Maybe next year we can find a better way,
To celebrate this very special holiday

Spring Time

Old man winter will soon be gone,
And we know that spring will soon come along.
Isn't it a wonderful sight to see,
When the beautiful light green leaves
return to the trees?
When the martins return to start building their nests,
And the yellow finches are our daily guests.
When the mocking birds
come with their beautiful song,
You just know that springtime has come along.
Springtime is a very special time of the year,
As everything seems to come alive and fill the heart with cheer.
The little yellow buttercups pushing their way through the sod,
reminding us of the faithfulness of our God.
For He is the one who gave us His Son.
To make a way for eternal life for everyone.
This is made sure when Easter comes,
And we all go to worship His resurrected Son.
Yes, springtime is a special time of year,
As all comes alive and our hearts are full of cheer.

Nature's Education or Early in the Morning

Early in the morning, after a long summer night is through,
the beautiful shining sun rays sparkle on the fresh fallen morning dew.
Sitting here in our water front home facing beautiful Tims Ford Lake,
Viewing nature's educational program of things only God could make.
A gentle breeze is blowing, making ripples on the clear blue water below.
Ducks of different colors and sizes are performing their daily show.
Swimming back and forth across the rippling water, chasing each other around and around, flapping their wings, bobbing their heads, and making their usual quacking sounds.
The martins are gracefully flying through the cool morning air, catching those tiny unprotected mosquitos that are completely unaware.
Here come the geese swimming down the lake, with several goslings in between.
This is an educational sight that most of us have seen.
A goose in front and a goose behind, keeping young goslings in a uniform line.
Nature is a master teacher, and her class room is open every day.
Waiting for her pupils to come out and hear what she has to say.
She teaches discipline, dedication, devotion, love and care.
And many other worthwhile subjects she graciously waits to share.
So arise, my friend, just past the break of day and enter mother nature's class,
you will find her teachings will brighten your day and last and last and last!

Hiram LeMay

The Flight of An Eagle

On top of a lofty mountain you will find the eagles building their nest.
A place to raise their young and find a place to rest.
What a beautiful sight it is for anyone to behold,
As they make that powerful leap into the air
and those magnificent wings unfold.
Watching them as they wing their way,
To the ocean below, seeking their food for the day.
And all of the sudden you see a great flash
As they strike the water with those steal like claws
Catching a salmon swimming by with vice like grip right under their jaw.
Turning as fast as a turbo jet back to their nest they go
to share the fish with the young eagles anxiously waiting there.
The flight of an eagle to the viewer seems to be a day of furor,
As he glides through the air seeking his prey.
But the eagle knows better, for he knows
He must find food for his young eagles every day.

Consider the Ant

I have read that verse so many times from Proverbs 6:6
And thought in my mind over and over again,
What does this verse really mean? Then one day it dawned on me,
Take God at His word go to the ant and see.
So, one day, to the woods I went, And there almost two hours I spent;
Watching those little creatures hard at work.
They were busier than a fast food store clerk.
It seemed as I watched them the best I could see,
Their home was in a hole at the base of a tree.
Back and forth I would watch them go . . .
Carrying food for the winter to their den to bestow
They would move so fast, not a one moved slow.
All had no trouble knowing just where to go.
I never saw one stop to play Or sit down along the way.
Sometimes their load was twice their size or more,
But they would always manage to get through the door.
Now I can say without any doubt,
I know for sure what Proverbs 6:6 is all about.
"Lord give me the strength of an ant," I asked.
Then I know I can finish each and every task.

Hiram LeMay

Autumn Scenes

Autumn scenes in Tennessee
Are beautiful to behold.
With sunbeams dancing on the leaves
Of red, green, yellow and gold.
In the late evening time,
When the sun is sinking low,
The colorful trees cast their shadows
In the still waters down below.
No artist could ever capture
the beauty that is seen,
As the colors mingle in the water so clear.
But we all know they will be back again,
In the autumn time next year.

The Election

The polls had closed and the announcement was made
That Bush was sure to win. But then we heard that history was on hold,
As all the votes were not in. Katherine Harris, Secretary of State, came forth
And reported the request was too late.
The hand counting was over, And Bush had won the race.
Then the Al Gore team came out in full force,
Just a few hours later they had reversed the course.
The counting restarted, and on and on it would go,
To prove what the record would finally show.
Days and weeks rolled swiftly by, Finally we heard the victory cry.
The counting is over and we are happy to present . . .
George W. Bush as our 43rd President.
While history was on hold what did we learn?
That the election process in our country needs to make a right turn.
For this is a much too important matter for any one state to hold,
Having the power of our elections to control.
Our legislative body should take a stern stand,
To see the proper voting machines are placed
In every county in our land.
Take action to eliminate the electoral college event,
And let the people of our land elect our President.
I feel sure if they take this action Before the 2004 election,
That the world would be told, History will not go on hold!

My Hobbies

Ages 12-87

I guess most of you already know by now that my favorite hobby is fishing. It all started when I was just about twelve years old when I had the first fishing trip with Granddaddy Morgan. Even though there was some things about that experience that I did not like, I did find it fun to sit, hold that pole, and watch that cork to see if it was going to go down.

On that particular trip it never did bobble, but on several trips with my Dad we caught buckets full of fish. I remember a trip that we made to Tunica Cut Off in Mississippi on a hot July day with not much wind blowing. We took plenty of water to drink and insect repellant to keep the bugs off. We arrived about 8:00 in the morning, put our flat bottom boat in the water, and started down the lake toward Dad's special fishing hole. We worked our way back through the willow trees, tied the boat to a limb, and started fishing.

I took along my fly rod made out of bamboo cane. Dad asked, "What are you going to do with that switch?"

I said, "I am going to catch me the biggest bream in this lake."

He replied, "You are fixing to lose that little pole. The fish in this lake will break that thing all to pieces."

Well, I got me a worm, put it on my hook, dropped it next to a stump in the water, and my cork never stopped. Down it went. The fish pulled my rod tip down and wrapped it around a willow tree, and broke it in two pieces. Dad just laughed, handed me a big heavy cane pole, and told me to get busy catching fish. That was some kind of experience for me as I had never seen bream that size before, but we had a full bucket by noon and headed home. Then came the fun—or hard work—of scaling and cleaning about fifty huge bream. The best of all was when Mother brought them out on a platter and placed them on the table with a bowl full of hush puppies and a big bowl of slaw.

Are you hungry yet? Well just give me a call, and I will get some out of the freezer, fry them up, and have them ready by the time you arrive.

Moving on to some of the other experiences that I have had through the years . . .

The first thing I had to do was save enough money to buy a new fly rod and remember never to use it at Tunica Cut Off. Let me say that I have not seen any bream as big as those we caught that day. Even though I have caught a lot of bream since then.

~~~~~~~~

There have been many different experiences that I have had on the water. Most have been wonderful, but some have been scary and very dangerous. Some have been very funny that could have ended up being a tragedy. One such time was when my son-in-law Bill Brewer and I went fishing at Woods Reservoir in weather conditions that were really not fit for even being outside must less on the water. Well the truth being we never got in the water as the temperature was below freezing, and the lake was frozen over. I backed the boat down thinking we might be able to break the ice with the trailer, but that did not work; and I tried to pull up to get the boat on level ground, and the ice on the ramp would not let me move. I just sat there and slipped on the ice trying to pull out, but it just would not move forward.

I told Bill to get the minnow bucket out of the boat, break the ice, and dip up water, and pour it under my wheels so I could get some traction. That is when things became so funny I could hardly stop laughing long enough to see how to drive the truck, as Bill was sliding all over the ramp. His feet looked like they were fixing to fly up over his head. Finally, I got enough traction to pull up off of the ramp. Bill was exhausted, and I was so tired from laughing that we thought we had just better head back for home.

Well you guessed it. I was never able to get Bill back in my boat in the winter time, and only a few times in good weather. That was a real turning point for him, and I believe it was not long after that experience that he took up golf. However, I have known the times when he would call me, and ask me to go play golf with him when it was so cold outside it would put frost on your nose, and your hands would be too cold to grip a club. I think he was just trying to get even with me. He never did say that was his reason, but I still have my doubts about that.

I do remember him going with me one time in my pontoon boat on Tims Ford Lake in good weather and having fun catching fish on the fly rod. He caught a bream, and a four pound bass chased it until he finally swallowed the bream, and Bill pulled him in. That was really a sight to behold, watching that bass follow the pontoon after that bream.

There are so many things that have happened when out on the water that I will never forget. When I was Pastor at Rugby Hills Baptist Church in Memphis, I had two experiences with two different members of our church. Andy Roe my Minister of Music and I loaded up the boat one morning and took off for Horseshoe Lake in Arkansas, about a two hour drive from where we lived. I told Andy that I was going to take him to my special place in the lake that was hard to get to but was full of big bream. I told him that I thought that I was the only one who ever fished in that place. That was something that I should have never said, as while we were sitting there fishing; Andy leaned over my shoulder and said, "You must have been drinking a lot of beer as there are beer cans all over the bank."

I had to let him know that I was wrong about no one else fishing in that place. Those cans were not mine. He couldn't wait to get back home and tell about the fishing trip and of course about what I had said about where we fished and what he saw. It was a long time before that

A Life of Miracles

one ever died down. Bro. Harber was another Minister of Music for us while I was there, and we had two trips that I will long remember. One was to the same lake where Andy and I fished—Horseshoe Lake in Arkansas.

We were on the west side of the lake under some Cypress trees fishing for those big bream, when a storm came up out of nowhere. I started up that little 5 horse power motor, and headed for the east bank as fast as that thing would go. But when we were about 15 feet from the bank, a tornado wind picked up our boat and set us down about 10 feet up the bank. Our equipment was scattered all over the ground, but thanks to the Good Lord neither one of us even received a scratch. We picked up what we could find, loaded up the boat, and headed home.

There were trees down and cars off in the ditch for a long distance on our way back home. Some roof tops were blown off and debris every where. We were so thankful to make it back home safe and sound. We were always hearing about bad storms in Arkansas, so it was a long time before we went back to Arkansas to fish even though it had some of the biggest bream that could be found that close to where we lived.

~~~~~~~~

The other experience that I had with Bro. Harber was also very scary but on a different lake. It was not about a storm but could have been worse. We were sitting under a cypress Tree fishing for bream in a flat bottom boat on Lake View in north Mississippi. That lake was full of big cypress trees. We would hold on to a limb, fish for a little while, and then move around until we found a bed of fish. Then we would tie the boat to a tree.

James was holding a limb until I could get the boat tied. I looked back in his direction, and happened to see that his hand was right in front of a cottonmouth snake that was lying on the limb asleep. I tried not to scare James, but as softly as I could speak I told him to move his hand off the limb as there was a big cottonmouth snake with his mouth about two inches from his hand.

He turned as pale as a ghost and said, "I can't turn loose of the limb. My hand is frozen to the limb."

I said, "Don't be afraid. Just slip your hand slowly off the limb." But he said, "I can't even move."

So I said, "Be still," and I crawled to the other end of the boat grabbed the snake behind its head and gave it a big sling into the water.

James said, "We are going to get out of here right now. I am so weak I can't sit up straight."

Well that ended that fishing trip, but we did have a ice chest full of big bream, so we just loaded up and took off for home.

I can remember several other times when I came close to being hit by another boater and three times caught out in the lake when a storm would come up. I was fishing on Old Hickory Lake by myself one day when a real bad storm came up out of nowhere, and I was about two miles down the lake from where I launched the boat. I took off as fast as I could go trying to make it to the dock before I was blown off the lake. I was only about one city block from the ramp, and there was two guys waving there arms for help. I just could not go passed them without pulling along side their boat to see what their problem was.

The wind was blowing at about 40 miles an hour, and the rain was pouring down. I gave them the end of a long rope and told them to tie it to something in the boat that was strong enough to hold, and I pulled them to the bank. They then helped me load my boat and were so thankful for me stopping to help. We had no more than loaded our boats until the center of the storm hit. Hail the size of golf balls were falling, and lightning was flashing all around. But we were all safe.

~~~~~~~~

Time continues to move along, and things keep taking place in my life that make me shake even now as I look back and realize how God has blessed and watched over me in so many experiences that I have had on the water when my life could have been wiped out. I recall the time when my son Mark was only about nine years old, and I had just bought a boat that I had been looking at for a long time. It looked so much safer than that little flat bottom I owned for years. It was a V shaped 16 foot with a cab that was half covered and a 20 horse motor. I decided to take Mark and go to Sardis Lake and try it out.

We arrived at the lake with not a cloud in the sky and hardly any wind at all. I knew that it was the time of the year when storms could come up at any moment, so I decided to go up stream in case a storm decided to move in. That was the direction from which most of the bad weather came. Well, that was a good decision, as we had gone about two miles up the river, and a dark cloud began to move overhead. I turned around, told Mark to get under the cab, and pull the canvas tarp I had in the boat over him while I tried to make it back to the ramp. The storm caught up with us and the waves on the water were so high, it was all that I could do to get the boat turned to the bank so we could get out and be safe. We were about one mile from the ramp when we finally got the boat to the bank, and lucky enough there was a small ditch running into the river, and I was able to run the boat a good ways into it where the boat would be safe there until the storm was over.

We stayed there under the tarp for about one hour until the storm passed. We were both soaked, but it was in July didn't take long to dry off. We made our way back to the ramp loaded the boat, and headed home without any other problems.

Mark looked up at me and said, "Daddy, I was scared." I said, "Mark, I was scared too."

We were so happy that we were in that V bottom boat instead of that flat bottom boat, as I don't believe we would have ever made it into the bank but would have been washed downstream and could have both been drowned. Praise the Lord for his love and protection once more.

~~~~~~~~

In the past five years it has been my good fortune to go to Melbourne, Florida for the winter where I could ocean fish from the beach and catch several kinds of good fish. This past winter was the best of the past five years there.

The main reason it was the best year of all is because the weather was nice every day, and the fishing was very good. I caught over 75 fish, cleaned them, and gave most of them to people who were not able to go fishing because of physical reasons.

We had several fish fries for our friends there in Melbourne. When we left there to go over to Okeechobee Lake, we spent three weeks with our friends Don and Loretta Brown who had a camp sight, and we gave all the fish in our freezer to the people in Melbourne.

A day's catch   Melbourne friends

Every day but one we would go out in the boat and troll for crappie and sometimes stop to fish for those big bream and shell crackers. We had a good place to stay there in Okeechobee. It was a fishing village called Stevens Winter Resort. Most of the people there were from Tennessee, and strange enough right here in the section where we live. They were all so friendly, and we all caught tubs of fish. I brought home two ice chests full of crappie and bream. I had two big fish fries there in the camp for our friends there, and four that came down to visit with us: Winston and Betty Randolph, George and Sherry Fitzgerald, and Don and Loretta Brown.

We ate several times with Don and Loretta while we were there and had a wonderful three weeks there in Okeechobee. I had long wanted to have the experience of fishing there, and it was a dream come true. We had several experiences while we were there.

One day a storm came up when we were about six miles up the river and barely made it back in time to load the boat and get it out before the high wind hit. One of the men that was out did not have it so lucky. The wind hit his pontoon, made it make a quick turn, and broke some ribs, messed up his shoulder, and threw his friend out of the pontoon into the river. He was very lucky and got out with out any real problems, but it could have been another real disaster as the river is full of huge alligators.

Jessie and I went down the river bank one day to fish for bream, and everywhere we would stop we would see those big alligators. I went down a pretty steep bank to find a place to fish, and Jessie hollered out, "Get back up the bank right now. There is a big alligator headed toward you." Well as you can see I made it or I wouldn't be telling about it.

My Hobbies

Ages 15-87

Now that you have sat on the bank of Nonconnah creek with me and followed the winding trail of adventure through the exciting years of my fishing experiences; hold on and go back to my younger days and take another sip of cold tea and take in the experiences of my hobby of golfing. I guess you could say that I got started about the age of 15 when my older brother Charley and two of our neighborhood friends decided to go over to the Pine Hill Golf course about two miles from where we lived. We signed up to be a caddy which was a different experience. We would leave home before day light and sign in before the others would arrive as it was first come, first out. We were given caddy badges to wear. My number was 364. When the Caddy Master would call out our number we would go to the club house and meet with the person that we would caddy for.

Well, that sounds pretty good but there was a lot that took place sometimes before we would be called. Some of the big bullies who came in late to sign up would try to make us let them put their names on the list ahead of ours. This is when the fight started and the Caddy Master would have to come to our rescue.

We would carry those heavy bags all day and make a big sum of $1.50. We would get a 10 cent tip if we did a good job and were able to find all the golf balls that the golfers would knock in the woods and high grass. After I had been caddying for awhile, the man that I caddied for asked me to be his special caddy. Because of this things got better for me. Some of the perks were I did not have to get up early to go to the golf course because he came by the house to get me. He would also bring me home. He paid me more than I would get if I stayed all day. Before I stopped caddying for him, he gave me some of his old clubs and balls. This is how I got my start in the hobby of golf. We had the privilege of playing on the course anytime except on weekends. A few times the four of us would go and hit balls with the clubs that I had been given and we would always find balls that others had lost.

As time moved on, my interest changed, and my golfing stopped until I reached the age of 32 and received my first set of clubs for my birthday from Shelbyville Mills Baptist Church when I was their Pastor.

I really became excited about the game of golf when I was in Shelbyville. Several men in our church liked to play, and we would play one day almost every week. There was only a hedge between my house and the golf course. I could just go through the hedge early in the mornings and start on number two hole, play nine holes, and be back in time for breakfast. On some of the rounds that I would play, the pro would go along with me and show me some things that would improve my game. He was such a big help that he had me shooting par golf in just a short time. He wanted me to enter a tournament that would be played with men of the town and thought I could do good. I knew they would play some on Sunday, and I told him that I could not do that. He said he would arrange it where I could play on week days, so I entered, as it did not cost me anything to play.

I had to play a man named Waterman who played golf almost everyday and was a real good golfer. I knew my chances of beating him were very slim, but to my surprise I stayed with him until the last hole where he beat me by one stroke. I was very proud to not get closed out before the end of the 18 holes. But that was my first time to ever play in any type of competition.

As the years passed by I had the opportunity to play in the preachers tournament at Henry Horton State Park where I won trophies every time I played. A few times they were for first place in my flight but several times in second or third place.

It was pleasure to play in the Georgia Preachers tournament three times and had the privilege of winning in my flight two times. The tournament was played at Callaway Gardens, a very beautiful course in LaGrange, Georgia.

I guess my greatest thrill came on January 15th in 1993 when I shot a hole in one at the New Blackberry Golf Course on Highway 231 between Shelbyville and Murfreesboro, Tennessee.

A Life of Miracles

Some of my friends that I played golf with every Tuesday were playing with me on this cold windy day in January: Willie Nelson, Hilary Dawson, John Smith and Tim Cunningham. Willie had hit his ball and had gone to the green. The other two had hit their shots, and now it was the old man's time. I got out my seven wood, reared back, and smacked the ball into the wind. The wind carried it to the hole and dropped it in the cup. A notice came out in the Shelbyville paper the next day, so it would be official.

LeMay scores hole-in-1 at Blackberry

From T-G staff reports

H.A. LeMay has become the first-ever golfer to score a hole-in-one on Blackberry Ridge's 125-yard No. 4 hole.

Willie Nelson, Tim Cunningham, John Smith and Hilleary Dawson witnessed the Jan. 15 achievement.

LeMay used a Giron club.

My Hobbies

Ages 25-65

I have always enjoyed working with wood and looked forward to the time when I could own all the tools to work with. I had the joy of having my mother live with us for seven years after Dad took his journey into his heavenly home; and I built her an apartment in two different places.

The first one was when I was Pastor Of Una Baptist Church, in Nashville. I went to Memphis and brought her back with me about 1976, as I did not think that the place she was living was safe. Then we moved to Grace Baptist Church in 1982, and I built her an apartment in our house on Old Dickerson Road where she stayed with us until Nancy had a sick spell in 1984. My brother Robert came and took Mother to live with him until she needed nursing home care. She stayed there until her death at the age of 101.

It was during the building of these two apartments that I had bought enough tools to get started doing some wood work for our Church at Una. With the help of some of our men we built a recreation hall on our new property. That called for a lot of wood work. I stayed up late many nights working on the building but learned a lot that helped me later on in life.

I began to make different things out of wood, sell them, and give the money to World Hunger as I always had a desire to help those in need. I made enough in a few years time to give a lot to World Hunger and buy several tools that helped me in the work when I moved from Grace to the last church that I pastored: Grace Baptist in Pleasant View, Tennessee.

The tools came in at a good time, as the church went into a building program, and I had the good pleasure of making several things for the new church building: a pulpit, two platform chairs, a communion table, and a table for our foyer. I also built the cabinets for our kitchen.

There was much work to be done, and it was a real pleasure to see the new church building sitting up on that beautiful hill, and seeing the people begin to come to worship with us. I was only able to stay there for three years, as Nancy was having some real health problems. So I had to take semi retirement, move out, and sell all my tools, as I knew I would not have time to use them any more. I found a place in Winchester, Tennessee while I was there helping the Grace Baptist Church while they looked for a pastor. We bought an old farm house and nine acres and moved there in 1992.

My Hobbies

Ages 68-87

My life at this age had taken a sudden change, and everything had to be centered around my wife Nancy, as she was having a difficult time with her health. We spent most of our time at the doctor's office or back and forth to the hospital. This of course brought about a change in my sports and hobbies. We did live close to the lake, and I did have a chance to go for a short period of time and catch a fish. I only played golf about twice in this period of time and had to retire from being pastor full-time. I helped several churches when they were without a pastor but could only do the preaching. I helped two churches for about a year, but I would only preach three times a week and helped one church with some visitation and funerals.

I had to sell all of my wood working tools and start doing craft work inside the house. I had some saw blades that I used with my wood work, and I started painting pictures on them and making clocks out of them. I would sell them and give the money to World Hunger and still do that until this day. It helped me to keep my mind busy and feel that I could still do a little to help people in need. Most of the clocks were sold in the churches that I served and some to friends of the members. I remember that it kept me pretty busy at Christmas time, as people would give them for gifts.

Nancy's health was getting worse by the day, and she had to have open heart surgery to repair a hole in her heart the size of a silver dollar. It was all down hill from there until she went home to be with the Lord on September 28th, 1998. We spent 58 wonderful years together. She was a wonderful mother, a devoted wife, and dedicated Christian. She fought a good fight and tried so hard to keep going but just did not have the strength. She was on oxygen day and night and spent her last nine days on a respirator.

It was a real challenge of my faith, but I could see the hand of God reaching out to make her completely whole. And He was right there to lead me through the valley of the shadow.

As David said in the Psalm 23, "Yea, though I walk through the valley of the shadow of death, I will fear no evil: for thou art with me; thy rod and thy staff they comfort me."

Now, stay with me as I turn back a few years and take you on a journey with me through our Ministry.

My Ministry

Ages 25-87

I feel that my ministry was filled with miracles. The first miracle took place in a cottage prayer meeting in 1946 as we were praying for revival to come to our church. I had been a member of Elliston Avenue Baptist Church for about three months leading the singing and teaching a Bible class when I came under conviction that I had not been saved but had just joined the church not understanding what it meant to really open my heart and receive Jesus as my Saviour. While I was praying it came to me very clearly that I needed to receive Jesus as my Lord and Saviour. I did just that and felt His presence come into my heart, and it has never left me. I knew then that I could sing, "Blessed assurance Jesus is mine."

I know that He has written my name in the Lamb's Book of Life in heaven and one day will call me home to be with Him forever. That took a miracle of love and grace.

When our third child was born, Dr. Birmingham told me that he would deliver that precious little baby girl, but God would have to give her life as that takes a miracle, and only God can give life. Even so with spiritual life, as only God can perform the miracle of the new birth.

In the third chapter of John, Jesus said, "Except a man be born again he cannot see the kingdom of God."

Nicodemus wanted to know how this could happen. Jesus answered his question in the 16th verse. "For God so loved the world, that He gave us His only begotten son, that whosoever believeth in Him should not perish but have everlasting life."

That same message is still there. Whosoever will call upon Him can receive everlasting life. That should be proof enough that God alone can perform the miracle of life. Now we will move on to the second miracle that took place in my life just a short time after the first miracle.

Stay with me now as we go to the miracle of my call into the ministry where many exciting things took place across the years.

After the cottage prayer meetings were over, our revival was started two weeks later. It was during this revival that I felt the call to preach the gospel. To me this was another miracle. I had not even finished high school, as World War II had started, and I knew I would soon have to go into service—an education of some sort but not what I needed for the ministry.

I was working at the Bluff City Buick Company in Memphis when I began to take courses through the mail but knew that I needed personal help. I began to pray that God would open the door for me to go to Nashville, Tennessee where I could attend Watkins Institute at night and work in the day. About two weeks after I prayed that God would open the door for me to go to Nashville, Mr. John Tune, owner of the Buick Company in Nashville, walked into our parts department. I heard him tell my boss, Mr. Fisher, that he was looking for a parts clerk. I had talked to Mr. Tune on the phone before about parts that he needed, so I knew his voice.

I was putting tail pipes in a rack, and I dropped them, ran to the front, and told him I would like to go to Nashville and work for him. My boss told me to get back there and put those tale pipes up, as I was not going anywhere. I told my boss the reason I needed to go, so Mr. Tune invited me to come up on the next Saturday, handed me a $20.00 bill, and told me to take the train that would bring me into the station in walking distance to his office.

I bought my train ticket, took off to Nashville, and walked over to Mr. Tune's office. In about thirty minutes I was on my way back to Memphis in a 1948 Roadmaster Buick to spend two more weeks with Bluff City Buick. Then I had my furniture sent to Nashville, loaded my family, and was on my way back to Nashville.

Mr. Tune said he would find me a place to stay, and he gave me $25.00 more than I was making. The 1948 Road Master was his personal car, but he gave me a 1939 Buick when I arrived and told me I could stay at his farm house located on the Harpeth River until I could find a place to live. He gave me two weeks to find me a place and look the city over before coming to work. That gave me a chance to go down the bank to the Harpeth in the afternoon and catch a few fish. All of this is just one more miracle.

Looking back just a moment, I would like for you to know the reason I am writing about this part of my life. The thought came to me that just maybe someone might read about how God had worked so many miracles in my life and maybe realize that He could do the same for them. I am sure there is someone out there that has said, as I did, I am not worthy to be a minister. But I have found that God can take some one like me who had so little to offer and use them for His glory even though we are not worthy.

I love the old song, "Little Is Much When God Is In It." I have found that to be very true. Paul said in 2nd Timothy1:12, "For I know whom I have believed and am persuaded that He is able to keep that which I have committed unto Him against that day." It is all a matter of being fully committed unto God that makes a difference in how our lives turn out.

After I answered the call to be a preacher, I was put to a test by my Pastor, Bro. J. C. Booth. He told me he wanted me to preach the following Sunday. Of course I told him I was not prepared yet. He said, "If God called you to preach, He will get you ready."

I was scared to death but began to get ready for the message. I remember so well what I Preached. Three points: Patch Up, Overhaul, or Make New. I called my brother-in-law, Shorty, who was not a Christian and asked him to come to the service. He came, and after the short message ended it was such a high spiritual time for me as Shorty came down to the altar, fell on his knees, and prayed words I will never forget.

"Lord, this is old Shorty. I have been such a sinner, but if You will save me, Lord, I will serve you the rest of my life." He got up threw his arms around my neck and said, "Thank God He saved me."

Well, Shorty did just what he said he would. He joined the Rugby Hills Baptist Church, became a deacon and Bible teacher up until the time God took him home. This was a wonderful blessing for me and for his family, as he was a heavy drinker; but he never took another drink after his experience of salvation.

I had asked God to save someone in that service, and He saved three. Praise His Holy Name. Another Miracle. This let me know without any doubt, that God had called me into the ministry.

~~~~~~~~

Well, we are now settled down in our cabin located on the beautiful Harpeth River where I can sneak down to river bank and catch a fish before dark. Looking each day for a place to rent, so we could move. I have been going each day to learn about the city of Nashville and how to find my way around. I have visited Watkins Institute and enrolled for the classes that I need to take to finish out my high school credits, so I can take a GED test and get ready for college in two years.

Time has moved along and we have found a place on Otter Creek Road in south Nashville for rent. We moved in but wished we had waited a little longer, as the water there was full of sulfur which stinks and turns everything black. I guess we put up with this long enough so I started looking for another place for us to live.

We joined Woodmount Baptist Church. Dr. G. Allen West was pastor, and they had a mission in an old Army base that had been turned into a housing project. I found a place there to move into and started leading the singing at the mission which was supported by Woodmount Baptist Church. Grady Randolph was the Pastor at the mission. My position was not a paid position, but I preached some for Grady and he would give me ten dollars. Probably that was more than it was worth. I not only led the singing but taught a men's Bible class which was a real joy.

I stayed very busy with my school work and my job at the church. I would get up every morning, go to work at 7:00 a.m., leave work, go to school, get out at 9:00 p.m., go home, and study until 12:00 a.m. I repeated this schedule four days a week for two years; but I worked six and a half days a week. When I finished there I went to Vanderbilt University and took the GED test and received my high school diploma. The dean told me that the psychology professor wanted to see me. Well, I went into his office. He said to me about being a minister, "I think you have chosen the wrong profession."

I said to him, "Sir, I did not make the choice. God chose me and promised to supply all of my needs."

I thanked him for his advice, but I don't think he understood what God could do with a person committed to do His will. I wish he could call me again after 62 wonderful years in the ministry and see what God has done with an uneducated country boy. I will tell more about that later.

My two years have come to an end at Nashville Motors. It is time now for me to move on to the next big step in my life. However, I would like to say that my two years with the Buick Company has been a wonderful experience for me as I have met a lot of wonderful people, and Mr. Tune has been very good to me. He knew from the beginning that I would only be with him two years, as I told him of my plan to enter college when I received my diploma. I went into his office and told him that I had enrolled in Cumberland University and would be leaving in two weeks. He had tried to get me to say that I would stay, as he wanted me to become Parts Manager, as Alvin who was parts manager was having to leave for duty in the Armed Services.

Prior to this time Mr. Tune sent me to a training school in Flint Michigan for Parts Managers. I had told him that he was wasting his money as I would not stay when Alvin left, but he just said, "I will take my chances."

Well, I boarded the plane and took off to Flint. When I arrived there I had one meal and got so sick that I had to be taken to the hospital where I stayed for two weeks, then flew back home, and never attended one class.

Several good things happened in the two years that I spent with the company. When I first went to work there I made it a point to tell all the fellow workers that I was a preacher, and would only be there two years. There were some pretty rough customers working there and at first tried to give me a hard time. I knew I had to do something to let them know that God loved them, so I took a 50 gallon oil drum into the men's restroom for a pulpit and had service every Tuesday at lunch time. I had an old Stella guitar that looked pretty rugged, and I took it to the meanest man in the shop and told him if he would paint it for me I would play them some songs.

He used a little of his rough language, which I will not repeat, but he said, "Bring it to me."

A Life of Miracles

Well he brought it to me painted a pearly white. It was so pretty. I put new strings on it, tuned it up, and took it with me into the restroom along with my Bible. I would sing a few songs, then take my Bible out and bring a message. Four of the men came to know Jesus through that ministry. I will tell you about one of the experiences. You don't want to put the book down now. This one is too good.

My Ministry

Concord Baptist Church

Graduation from Belmont 1954

Concord Baptist Church

Several years after I left the Buick Company and had gone to college at Cumberland University in Lebanon, I moved back to Nashville and entered Belmont College to finish up my college work. After I had become the pastor of Concord Baptist church in south Nashville, one night about 11 o'clock my phone rang. It was a man that used to work at Nashville Motors when I was there. He was crying so that I could hardly understand what he was trying to tell me, but he finally let me know that he wanted me to come to his house. He said that he had killed his wife.

I started to tell him that he needed the police not a preacher, but I asked for his address, put on my clothes, and took off to West Nashville. When I arrived at his home, he was sitting on the front porch crying. He looked up and said, "I didn't know who to call for help, but I remembered you from being at Nashville Motors, and that you were a preacher, and thought you might come and help me.

I asked him how his wife died, and he said, "I killed her, not with a gun, but with my drinking. She was such a good wife. She went to church and prayed for me all the time, and I just would not stop my ways. She died from a broken heart over the way I lived. I would like for you to tell me how I can get right with God, so I can go where she has gone."

I took the Bible and went through the plan of salvation with him and ask him to pray the sinners prayer with me if he wanted to be saved. So we got on our knees on the porch, and he followed me in the sinners prayer. I told him that now that he had received Jesus as his Saviour, that he needed to find a church home, follow the Lord in baptism, and serve the Lord.

He said he would do that and thanked me for coming. The thought came to me as I was leaving his home of a poem that I had read years ago . . .

> Drop a pebble in a brook; a splash, and then it is gone;
> But there are a hundred thousand ripples
> circling on and on and on.
> When we drop a kind word for Jesus,
> and tell people of God's love;
> There is a chance that they will believe in Him,
> and be ready for their home above.

God's word tells us in 1Corinthians 3:6, "I have planted, Apollos watered; but God gave the increase."

To God be the glory for the things He has done!

~~~~~~~~

Before I move on to other experiences of my ministry, I want to share a few other things that took place while I worked at Nashville Motors.

Several years later I was visiting some sick people at Baptist Hospital. As I was walking down one of the halls I saw this man standing with his hands over his face. He looked like someone that I had seen before. I placed my hand upon his shoulder. He looked up, threw his arms around me, and said, "Preacher LeMay!" I said, "Horace Mitchell who worked at Nashville Motors in 1948." He said, "I am so glad to see you." As he wiped tears from his eyes, he told me that his wife had just received bad news from a test they had run. They said she had cancer that was wide spread. "I don't know what to do," he said. "I don't even know how to pray." I invited him to go with me to the prayer room.

"I would like that," he said. I told him that he could find strength in the Lord if he knew Him. He said, "I guess you know that I am not a Christian." I told him that I did not know, but would be willing to tell him how he could become a Christian. He said, "Please do." I gave him the plan of salvation and asked him if he would like to follow me in praying the sinner's prayer. Without hesitation he said, "Yes I would." We got down on our knees, and he prayed the sinner's prayer. I said, "Now you can call upon Jesus to give you the comfort that you need for the days ahead." I had prayer for his wife. He thanked me for being there when he needed someone so bad.

One other thing that I should have said earlier was the last conversation that I had with Mr. Tune. Mr. Gant, the book keeper, brought me my last check and told me Mr. Tune wanted me to stop by his office before I left. I stopped by, and he asked me again if I would stay. I told him how much I appreciated everything he had done for me, but the decision was not mine. I was doing what I was sure God wanted me to do. He said, "I appreciate what you have meant to our men here in the shop."

He handed me a check for $500.00 and said that was for my books that I would need, and there was a blank check in his desk if I ever needed help. Of course you know I was overcome, and with tears in my eyes I received the check but glad I never had to ask for more.

My Ministry

Hopewell Baptist Church

It is time to load up and take off for some new adventures. Tighten your seat belt and hold on, as we make our way to Lebanon Tennessee and to Cumberland University where I will start taking classes next Monday after we move into our apartment on back of the campus. When we left Nashville we had to sell our first home. That was so hard to do, as we loved it so much, but it had to be done in order to have money to start over in Lebanon.

We arrived there on Monday afternoon and tried to get everything set up before I walked up the path to the University to sign up for my classes that would start the next Monday. Would you believe that late that afternoon I had a phone call from some friends that I met when I was a member of Woodmount Baptist Church in Nashville. They wanted to know if I would go to Hopewell Baptist Church and preach for them as they were without a pastor. Here I was just arriving in Lebanon, and the Lord was there to open a door for me to preach. So I said I would go. I loaded up Nancy and the kids and took off for my mission.

The church was located on the Sumner and Trousdale County lines, down a dirt wagon trail that led through a creek with running water. The church building looked to be over a hundred years old with a huge rock sitting next to the front doors. There were two front doors. The women would enter the one on the right, and the men would go in the one on the left in the years gone by; and the big rock was left there for Aunt Bessy to ride up to it and get off of her horse so she wouldn't fall getting off the horse. It had become a sacred rock and was not to be removed, as I tried after being there about six months. I guess it is still there today even though the church has closed the doors for good.

Well, I went in to find just about 10 people waiting to hear this new preacher boy. I preached like the house was full and was soaking wet when I finished. They ask me to come back on the next Sunday. I accepted their invitation. The deacons, three in number, wanted to talk with me after the service. They ask me if I would be willing to become their pastor, and they would pay me $17 a week. It was 17 miles from the University to the church, and that was one way. So I guess they were giving me 50 cents a mile. Whatever, I am sure I was not worth that much.

After we had our meeting with the three deacons, the chairman Brother Echols invited us home for dinner. Dear Bro. Jim and his sweet wife, Matty, had really put the little pot in the big one. It had been a long time since I had seen that much food on a table that I was invited to visit. I'm not sure if I ever saw one with that much food. While we were eating Mrs. Matty was circling the table telling us to "make out our dinner." That meant, "Keep eating." Then she brought in the pie, cake, and home made ice cream. This young preacher boy really got his fill, as did my family.

They showed us a room in their house, and said, "This is your room. You can stay here any time you like."

And we did stay there several times while I was their pastor. After being there about three weeks, I asked them if they would like to have a revival. I told them that we would need to set up a time to make a survey of the community and make some personal calls after the survey. One of the men spoke up and said that he knew everybody in that community, and it would be a waste of time. But the other six or seven said, "Let's go for it."

Well we made the survey, and old Zack was most surprised at the people he did not know. There was a student in Cumberland named Roy Dispaine, who was studying to become a Minister of Music. He agreed to lead the music for us.

Another boy, Kenneth Floyd, an excellent piano player, said he would play for our revival. We had a wonderful 10 day revival, and 22 people were saved and joined the church. We had baptism in Bledsoe Creek where I baptized Sanders Lackey, the first convert that we had before the revival. He was saved in January and wanted to be baptized the next week. So we went to Bledsoe Creek broke ice and had frozen baptism service. We both came up with icicles hanging off our clothes and thankful neither one of us got sick.

One of the men of the church asked, "What are we going to do with all these new people?"

My reply was, "God gave them to us, and He will lead us in taking care of them."

So we began to revise the inside of the building and hung curtains up to make class rooms for Bible study. Before the first year ended, we were having 55 people in church and about 45 in Bible study.

There were so many experiences at Hopewell in the short period of time that I was there, and several at the University as well. At the church there were several experiences that will always be remembered. Even though the church never gave me much money, they did give me the opportunity to do what God called me to do—preach the word. They also gave my family lots of love.

Just about twice a month I would have trouble finding room in the back seat of that 1940 Chevy for my two children, as the people would load it down with food. The only time that we ran out of food and money was when the ice storm hit. It lasted for two weeks, and no one could get out. I walked up to the library at the University, got on my knees, and ask God for help. My children were getting cold as our oil was running low, and old mother Hubbard's cabinet was empty.

As I came out of the library to go back down to the house, the lady that stayed in the Post Office saw me and said, "Wait. I have a letter for you."

She handed me the envelope that had only my name on the outside. There was no message inside, but a five dollar bill that looked a foot long. I don't know even to this date who gave me the money, but I am sure it was an answer to prayer.

I got home as fast as I could to share the good news with my wife. I bought a dollar's worth of oil for the stove, got a friend to take me to the store, as he had chains on his car, and I bought $4.00 worth of food—beans, oats, and milk. That lasted until the ice melted, and I could make it back to the church where my car was loaded again with food, and we could get back to normal.

I will always remember the Indian lady named Lena Pedigo who lived with her mother and father in a shack back in the woods. She would walk to the creek, sit on a stump, and wait for me to pick her up when the creek was up and running. Some times she would take off her shoes and wade across if the water was not to deep. Her mother and father never came to church, but Lena was there every Sunday. It was a pretty long walk from her shack to the creek, but she would even come when it was raining. She loved to hear Mrs. Scott play the old pump organ. One of her grandsons would pump the peddles while she played. It had a real sweet sound.

This was so funny . . . One of the men of our church gave his wife a vacuum cleaner for her birthday, but when she went to use it he told her she couldn't do that for it would use too much electricity. HA. HA.

Not long after that experience, old Brother Zack got sick. I went by his house to see him, and he was all leaned back in his easy chair sipping on hot cup of coffee. I think he had a bad case of the flu, so I didn't want to tarry too long. We talked for a while, and then I told him I wanted to read a few verses of Scripture for him. The room was so dark that I could not see to read. I asked him where the light switch was located. Would you believe he told me to just move over closer to the window as there was still a little daylight left?

Well, I moved over, read a few verses from the Bible, and had prayer for him. Before leaving the house I made a BIG mistake. I asked him if I could help him do anything. He turned to me and said, "Be here at 6:00 in the morning. There are thirty cows that need to be milked. I had never milked that many cows, but I milked our one cow many times. So the next morning I showed up and went out to the barn and milked those thirty cows. My arms and fingers cramped the rest of the week. I could hardly turn the pages in my Bible on Sunday morning, but I would never have told the people why I was having trouble, as our church had nothing but farmers. I learned a great lesson that night I stopped by to see old Lack—be careful what you say you are willing to do even though you would like to be helpful.

Lack had a son named Clarence. His wife was a member of the church and had asked prayer for him many times. I made it a point to go visit him one day, and his wife told me he had just left to go check on his sheep as the vultures were flying around in circles over the hill where they were. That was a great experience for me. As I went up that big hill to find him, he was spreading salt on the ground and calling his sheep so he could see if any were missing. Well the sheep started coming in from every direction, and I noticed that Clarence was busy counting. He didn't even know that I was around. He stopped counting, and I walked up and introduced myself to him. He told me that two of his sheep were missing.

It looked to me like there were at least 100 sheep in the fold.

I asked Clarence if he would like to sit on that big old rock and talk. He said he would after he found the two sheep that were missing. So here we go through the woods looking for the two lost sheep. We finally found them, or what was left after the vultures had finished with them.

We went back and sat down on the rock, and I said, "Clarence, I have just seen the Scriptures come alive. You know how many sheep you have in your fold, and Jesus knows how many there are in His fold. He calls us his sheep, and He even knows us all by name. One day He promised to come and take us home with Him, where we would be free from all the vultures in this life. Would you like to be one of God's sheep, Clarence?" He said, "How can I do that?" I turned to the book of Romans and read God's plan of salvation with Clarence looking over my shoulder. Then I said, "Clarence, if you are ready to ask God to forgive your sins and receive Jesus as your Saviour, you will become one of the sheep in God's fold." He agreed to repeat the sinners prayer after me. That whole hillside seem to light up as that big man stood up with tears in his eyes, lifted his arms up toward heaven, and said, "Thank you, God, for letting me enter your sheep fold." Then he turned to me and thanked me for coming to share God's Word with him and said, "Let's go down to the house and tell my wife."

That was another happy experience as they were so happy that God had given them a Christian home to bring up their baby that God had just given them. Clarence promised to start attending church, and he did. He was there every Sunday while I was there as Pastor and was asked to be a deacon before I left. This is the type of experience that means more to me than all the money in Fort Knox.

It was not long after this experience that Tennessee Baptist bought Belmont College in Nashville, and we had to leave Lebanon. We had to choose where we would continue our education. This was a real problem, as we all had families, and had to find a place to live. We spent a lot of time trying to find a place to live, before we finally settled in Nashville in an old house on the back of Belmont campus. Another preacher and I moved our families in. John Cavanaugh went up stairs, and I took the down stairs as I had more children.

Nancy, me, and our five children

My Ministry

Concord Baptist Church

I continued to drive back and forth to Hopewell for about six months and was contacted by the Concord Baptist Church in Nashville to come and preach for them, as they were without a pastor. When I went the next Sunday and preached for them, they asked me to be their pastor. I accepted their call. I went back to Hopewell for two more weeks to give them time to seek another pastor.

The first Sunday that I went back to Concord as their pastor, my family was invited to have dinner with the Waller family. Brother Jim was the chairman of the deacons, and his wife Martha was a member of the Methodist Church in Nolensville, just a few miles up the road. She had prepared a wonderful meal for us. I ate so much that when she brought out that big beautiful coconut cake, I told her that I could not eat another bite, but if she would cut me a slice I would take it home for my supper. Well, brother Jim looked at me and said, "Preacher, let me get one thing straight with you right now (in tones that sounded like an army drill sergeant). You can eat all you want to here, but you can't take anything home with you."

I almost melted in my chair. When he saw that I looked like I was going to pass out, he told his daughter to go wrap up a piece of that cake and bring it to the preacher. I sure was relieved. I was still living in the house on Belmont Campus and stayed there until we could build a parsonage. After about six months we were able to move into the parsonage that all of the men of the church, including the pastor and some of the women, had built. We had to haul in dirt to put on top of the hill where the parsonage was to be built, because Mill Creek flooded that area after a big rain. We had only been in the house just a short time when the big one came along.

I was at Belmont in class, when I received word that Mill Creek had already gone over the banks and was rising fast. So I jumped in my car, drove as fast as I could, and stopped by a friends house to pick up his flat bottom jon boat. I put the boat in the water that had already come up to the Nolensville Road, jumped in the boat, and paddled about 300 yards up to my back door steps, went in, and found a note on the table. "We have gone to higher ground."

It was such a relief to know my family was safe. It took the rest of the week to clean the church building as water had flooded the sanctuary with about three feet of muddy water. We were really happy that the water did not get in the house and so happy that we had put the extra dirt on the hill where the parsonage was built.

Mill Creek did run high a few times after that but never flooded again while we were there. We have many fond memories of the time we spent there. Every year we would have a big dinner on the church lawn overlooking Mill Creek. People would bring their hay wagons and use them for tables. There would always be enough food to feed a small army. We would go inside after dinner and listen to several quartets the rest of the day.

That was a very happy time as former members who had moved away would come for the outing. It was the Sunday following the home-coming that Mrs. Waller became a member of our church, and Brother Jim was very happy.

I had an old Kaiser auto that I would use to round up several kids on Sunday morning and bring them to Sunday School. I recall being told about a man that lived back in a wooded area that never came out in the day time, so I thought I would go down that long dirt road and meet him. I went as far as I could in that old Kaiser, but it got too rough, and I had to get out and start walking. I had not gone very far until I heard the sound of someone cutting wood. I looked through the trees and saw this little man who was very short and skinny swinging a big ax. I walked up beside him and told him who I was, and he said, "I don't need to talk to you."

I said, "You look tired. Why not just sit here on this log and rest a few minutes."

To my surprise he did. He told me that the reason he never went out in the day time was because he thought he might be caught as he had killed a man in self-defense and thought he might be put in jail.

He had a wife and daughter that lived in a shack that he had built that he needed to take care of.

I read some Scriptures to him and ask him if he would like to receive Jesus as his Saviour. He did and prayed the sinner's prayer with me. I went and did some checking about his case, and found it had been dismissed. I went back and told him. The next Sunday he and his family were in church, and all came forward for baptism. They were very faithful members as long as I was there.

I looked out my window one Sunday morning and saw Mr. Fuller's truck in the church yard. I went over and asked why he was there so early. He said, "My brother is coming to see me, and if I am there I will have to miss church. I left him a note and told him I was at church." What a testimony.

There were many different experiences that took place while we were pastor at Concord Baptist Church near Nolensville, Tennessee. It had a history that dated back before the Civil War. There were records kept that I had the privilege of reading. The writing was done with a goose quill and was so beautiful. There was one very interesting page that told about the man who gave the property where the church was built. He was Dr. Lafeet Ezell. He had been caught having a relationship with one of the women in the church. He was requested to come for a meeting with the deacon body and refused to come, so his name was removed from the church roll. That was back when church discipline was carried out.

You either repented or got put out. I will never forget that horrible day. We were busy working on the parsonage when a car pulled up to the house, and Bill Puckett jumped out of the car crying so hard that you could hardly understand what he was saying. He had just received word that the girls' basketball team was playing, and several of the girls were rushed to the hospital. One was his daughter. I changed my clothes and took off to the hospital as fast as I could go, and found out that an epidemic of polio had hit the team. Three had died, and the others were in critical condition.

Even to this day you can see Billie Puckett on a TV commercial that is advertizing Scooters. She is still living, and last I heard she is still working for the Baptist Sunday School Board.

Well it was not long after that I was asked by some men of the church to go rabbit hunting with them early the next morning. Well, about two in the morning my brother had to rush me to the hospital with painful cramps. About six o'clock he came back in my room and told me that we had a baby girl up stairs. They had given me a shot, and I was feeling much better, so I jumped out of bed put on my clothes, and took off up stairs to welcome Bonnie Dell into our family. Of course I had to fight off the nurses that were trying to get me back in bed. I never had another pain, and Nancy said it was the easiest delivery she had ever had. I believe until this day that I went to the hospital to have the birth pains for her.

My experiences at Concord were different than any other church that I served. I had some wonderful times with some wonderful people in those years from 1951 to 1954, but the church field was very limited for future growth at that time. We had seen the church make some real progress in those four years, as the number of members had grown from 80 to 150, and I had been in every home in that community several times. We had built a parsonage and added several class rooms and a kitchen to the educational building.

My Ministry

Una Baptist Church

I received a call from the Una Baptist Church that was located on Murfreesboro Road. The community was one of the most rapidly growing areas in Nashville at that time and gave me the privilege of ministering in a community that had a much larger population. That gave me a better chance to reach more people with the Gospel. Their building was old and in much need of being replaced, but I knew it would take a lot of hard work. It only had about two acres of ground. In the back of the church building there was a big gully, and on the north side even a larger gully. Both needed to be filled in before we could start a building program.

In one year we had grown from 146 to 250 people and were out of space in the sanctuary, and educational building. We had one class of boys meeting in the small kitchen. We even had to use some hall space for a class room. Our church was in third place in Tennessee Baptist

Convention baptisms that year, and we were in the top ten the rest of the time that I was their pastor.

We had a couple that visited our church every year on their way to Florida. They said they stopped there because they knew they would receive a Gospel message. They also said they were afraid the floor would cave in before they could get out of the building as it was so shaky. The church decided it was time to get started filling in the gullies and get ready to build. So we hired a contractor and found a bond company that helped us with the finances. We started selling bonds, and after we sold two hundred and fifty thousand dollars, we got started with the new building. A few months later we were in our new building.

The people that stopped by every year acted as happy as all of our people over the building and enjoyed being there for our big dinner in our new fellowship hall. In seemingly about six months we were in our new facilities and there was room for growth. In about one year we had grown from 250 membership to 475. There were many things that took place at Una Baptist while I was there that were wonderful experiences and some very funny.

One time I was coming from the baptistry and two of my deacons were standing at the door entering the sanctuary waiting to do their usual thing and asked me some crazy questions. The question this time was, "We would like to know why you kneel at the pulpit and you did not kneel in the baptistry?"

These two deacons that kept doing these tricks were Wyman Creech and Hershell Merriweather. I love them both. They kept me on my toes.

Another funny experience came about when a young boy named Figg Newton was being baptized. I asked him several times what his real name was, and he insisted that it was Figg Newton. You can imagine what happened when I said, "I baptize thee Figg Newton." At this time I lost the congregation as they burst out in laughter, and I said, "This is the first time that I ever baptized a cookie."

I must say in all of my experiences there was only one other that brought the congregation to laughter and that was when I baptized this lady that weighed over 250 pounds. She pulled me backward in the water on top of her, threw me about two feet in the air, and came up shouting. Now that is real baptism.

A Life of Miracles

~ ~ ~ ~ ~ ~ ~ ~

Moving on in our experiences at Una Baptist Church . . .

One of our beautiful young girls was rushed to Baptist hospital at 11:00 one night for surgery, so I got dressed and took off to the hospital. When I arrived, Patricia was in real bad pain, crying, and asking, "Why am I having to go through this surgery?"

I had prayer with her, and told her that she was in God's hands, and she would be all right. After I talked with her for a little while, a lady came into the room who was related to the Briggs family. She had been told that a minister was in the room with Patricia, and she came to see if I would go to the room where her father was and have prayer with him, as she was not sure if he was a Christian. I went to his room and asked him if he was a Christian. He could not talk but shook his head no. I took his hand and ask him if he wanted to be a Christian, and if so to squeeze my hand twice. He did so, and I asked him to follow me in the sinner's prayer in his heart, and told him to squeeze my hand three times if he was receiving Jesus as his Saviour.

He followed me in prayer, looked up with tears running down his cheeks, and squeezed my hand three times. I was so happy, but tired, and had a busy day coming up, so I took off home. Returned the next morning to visit Patricia and found her propped up in the bed with a big smile on her face. As soon as I walked into the room she told me that she had heard the good news about the man that raised her mother and was so happy. She said anytime God wants me to have surgery I will not question why, as her grandfather who died that night would not have been saved.

Patricia married a preacher a few years later, Bro. Joe McGeehe, who passed away at the age of 43. I conducted his funeral. I was in revival with a preacher friend and told about this experience, and some other experiences that I will write about later. He said to me, "You need to write a book as the Lord has blessed you with so many experiences that many people would love to read about."

This was about 1966, and I am just now getting around to putting some of them on paper. I do hope they will be a blessing to all who have a chance to read this book.

Patricia and Joe had two boys. The youngest, named Tim, is now preaching at the Grace Baptist Church in Tullahoma, Tennessee. His father was a preacher and also his grandfather, so God continues to use that family to reach lost souls for His kingdom.

I have had so many experiences with this family. I have been with Tim in revival at the First Baptist Church in Chapel Hill, Tennessee where Tim got his start. He did such a good job there that God moved him to Grace in Tullahoma where he could reach more people, and he is doing just that. I recall the time when Griffin Briggs, Patricia's father came forward in a service at Una Baptist one Sunday morning at the invitation time and ask for prayer. He said he needed to rededicate his life to the Lord. Two weeks later he was rushed to the hospital with a massive heart attack and died just a few days later at the age of 43. I believe he had a feeling that he was fixing to leave planet earth when he came forward in the church service. I had his funeral service three days later. Griffin was the general manager of Nolen Tank Company in Nashville, and the company had sent a flower arrangement made like a water tank that was placed at the foot of his grave sight. There was a flower arrangement in a four foot cross at the head of the grave sight. The wind was blowing so hard, that just as I finished the prayer at the grave sight, the tank was blown over by the wind, but the cross was still standing. As I looked up and saw what had happened I said, "His work has been finished, but his life goes on," pointing to the tank on the ground, "and the Cross still standing."

I made the statement that Griffin made to me just two weeks before he died. "He would like to have the privilege of leading someone to Jesus; and even though he did not live long enough to see that take place, just maybe there is someone hear today that has been touched by his life that would like to come forward and receive Jesus as your Saviour in answer to his prayer."

An elderly man came forward from the back of the crowd and said, "I would like to receive Jesus as my Saviour, as this man has meant so much to me; and I want to go where I can be where he has gone."

Well, as you would know there was not a dry eye in that crowd; and I believe they were tears of Joy. Strange things were taking place as we witnessed God's marvelous grace taking place before our very eyes.

I served Una Baptist Church from 1955 until 1959 and then again 1970 until 1982, making a total of 16 years my longest pastorate of any of the seven churches that I pastored full time. I was at Grace

Baptist in Nashville twice, 1967-1970 the first time, and 1982-1988 for a total of 11 years. I served those two churches a total of 27 years. So the experiences from these two churches were more in number than the other five churches.

As I continue my ministry with the Una Baptist Church it will include both of the times that I served them as pastor. It was not long after we moved into our new building that I answered the call of Shelbyville Mills Baptist Church in December 1959. The experiences that I have just given were in the first four and a half years as pastor of Una.

I will move on now to the last 11 years. I had not been back but about five years when a tornado came through and destroyed our building. We were in the old building having a meeting with the church council when I heard this loud sound—like a freight train—and I told everybody to hit the floor and crawl down the steps to the basement, as the lights had gone out. The lightning flashed, the thunder rolled, and the rain poured for about 10 minutes. When it stopped I went upstairs to see what had happened. The lightning was still flashing, and I looked out the front door window and saw one of the ladies' cars had the glass broken out. When I told her what I saw she moved toward the door and said, "I know it is April Fool's Day."

When she looked out, a flash of lightning lit up the whole area, and she screamed out, "The top of our church building is in Smith Springs Road." We just stopped, had prayer, and gave thanks to our blessed Lord that we were all safe though very sad.

Electric wires were flashing so I told everyone to be careful and try to make it home to see if all was well with their families, and I would do the same. I knew there was not anything that could be done until the next day.

A miracle took place as we were to have a revival that week, and several people would have been killed. There were concrete blocks in almost every seat. We had just changed our revival date two weeks before, at the request of our association, to participate in the simultaneous revival. If that was not a miracle then I don't know what a miracle is.

Well, next we met with the deacons at the old building to make plans for getting things back in shape. We called our insurance company, contacted our contractor, and got things started in rebuilding. We then contacted the Una School Board to see if we could have our services in the school until we could get back in our building. They were very nice and said we could do that.

We contacted our evangelist and told him what had happened, and that we would be having the revival in the Una School Building. Bro. Frank Kellogg was the pastor of Una at one time and was happy that we were going to have the revival and that the church had asked him to be the evangelist. We had a wonderful revival, and many souls were saved. I believe the tornado helped in getting our people ready for revival.

It was only a few months until we were back in our building and began to grow so fast we had to make plans to find some property so we could relocate and build again. We found a five acre tract, just across Murfreesboro Road in back of our present property and voted to buy the property and make plans for the building program. About one month later we were breaking ground for the new building.

We had listed our present building for sale, and it sold with stipulations that we could remain there until our building was completed. Everything just seemed to fall in place, and we were able to move into our new building and have our dedication service in a very short period of time. I have a video that was taken of this event that I wish I could show you the happy faces of our people as we marched across the road to the new building and share with you the wonderful meal our ladies had prepared. That was such a wonderful day, and God had blessed us once again.

The new church was very attractive, and caught the eye of all the new people moving into our area. It was not long until we were having 450 people in service. We had enough property to build a recreation building in the back of the property, a play ground, and a ball field for the little children. This all took a lot of man hours, as we cut trees into stove wood and sold the wood to help pay for the building material for the recreational area. The church building was an all—purpose building with a full-sized skating rink and a full-sized kitchen in the basement that we used to give the children a place to come after they got out of school and before their parents arrived from work.

~~~~~~~~

Before moving on to my next pastorate, I will share some more of the experiences that took place at Una in the 11 year period. One day after I had spent about two hours in study and prayer I went out to make some visits in our community and had some visitor cards that had been turned in the past Sunday. When I got in my car to go to one of the homes on one of the cards, I just kept getting the feeling that I should be going to another street, so I changed directions, and started down a street that I did not have a card for. Driving very slowly, I saw a lady standing on her porch crying. I pulled up into her driveway, got out, went up to her porch, told her who I was, and asked if I could be of help to her.

She said, "Please come in, as I need help."

She told me that her husband lost his job and was out looking for work, and their baby was sick and she didn't have any money to take her to the hospital. I asked her if she was a Christian, and she said, "No," but she would like to know how she could become a Christian.

I took the Scriptures and showed her how to receive Christ. We had the sinner's prayer and she accepted Jesus. We went back into the room where the baby was and had prayer for the baby. I told her I had some other visits that I had to make, but that I would get back with her later in the day. After several visits I returned to church for lunch. I had not been there long until Elizabeth called and said that Charlie was back home and wanted to talk to me.

I ate a bite of lunch and went back to find them rejoicing, as the baby's fever had gone and Charles had found a job. He told me that he would also like to know how to become a Christian. It only took a few minutes until we were on our knees praying the sinner's prayer, and Charlie was up rejoicing. They both were in church the next Sunday and were baptized that Sunday night, and became some of the most faithful members. They later moved to Rover, Tennessee, and he became a deacon in the First Baptist Church there. As far as I know he is still living there and serving the Lord. I have often said that was one of the divine directed visits that I had experienced, but it was not the last one. Just another miracle. One day I visited in the home of a lady who had been visiting our church, and she had told me that she wanted to join the church but was waiting for her husband to go with her. She had told me when I could catch him at home, so I would know when to visit. Well I went at the time she told me, and he was there. I told him who I was and why I had come. He said he was too busy to talk to me as he had to go back to work. I tried to get him to stay there for just a few minutes so I could talk to him about our church, but he was too busy, and I didn't want to make him mad. So I handed him one of my business cards and told him if he ever found time to talk with me to give me a call. He thanked me, put the card in his pocket and left.

I guess it had been about two months when he called me one night about 11:30 and told me with his voice breaking up that he was in Vanderbilt hospital and told me the room number where he was. I put on my clothes and took off to the hospital arriving about midnight. He was standing outside his wife's room crying. I walked up, placed my arm around his shoulder, and asked him what I could do.

He turned to me and said, "You told me if I ever needed you to call you. I found your card in my wallet and started not to call, but I needed you so bad I thought I would see if you could come. The doctor just gave me some bad news about my wife, and I had told her that I would tell her when he came and gave me the report. I just can't do that and thought maybe you would tell her for me."

I said, "I don't think that I should be the one to tell her, but I believe if you will trust the Lord he will give you the strength."

He said, "But I don't know the Lord."

Then I told him how to be saved, and he prayed with me the sinner's prayer.

I told him that now we will go into her room and trust the Lord to take care of the results, so he agreed. We went into the room, and he sat down by the bed, and took her hand. She looked up and saw the tears in his eyes and said, "Honey, you don't have to tell me anything. I already know."

He bowed his head and said, "Thank You, Jesus," and told his wife about the decision that he had made and said, "We will go to church together when you are able."

They went home the next week and came to church and were baptized that night. Mabel had terminal cancer and only lived about three weeks. She said, "Now I can go happy, for I know we will meet again."

There were so many experiences that took place while I was pastor at Una, I will not try to tell about all of them, but there are a few more that I feel like sharing with you, so just rear back in that big easy chair and take another sip of that cold glass of tea. You should lay a towel in your lap, as this next event may bring a tear to you eyes, as it has for me just reliving this part of the ministry at Una.

We had a bus ministry headed up by Bro. Marvin Jarvis who took care of the five buses, and I mean in every way. They were always having work that needed to be done, and he kept them serviced. Many times in the cold winter weather, I would go to the church and find him laying on the cold ground under one of the buses fixing something that had quit working or putting on some part that needed to be changed. He also went out every Saturday morning to visit in the homes of the children on his route.

There was one little boy, Dwight Morris, who gave Bro. Jarvis a lot of trouble. Many times I would see him with Dwight under his arm giving him a spanking for acting up on the bus. We had children's church downstairs in the basement, and they had to stay there until they were ready to come upstairs and worship. Dwight finally became calm enough to join us in worship.

One Sunday morning, Dwight came into my study and asked if he could lead in prayer in big church? I was really surprised that he had made that much spiritual growth since he had received Jesus as his Saviour. I told him to just wait and go to the pulpit with me, and I would let him open the service in prayer. I have never heard a sweeter prayer from the lips of an 11 year old boy.

When he finished my eyes were running with tears, and it looked like everyone in the congregation was wiping tears from their eyes. It was only a short time after that experience that Dwight died with Downs Syndrome. I feel sure that when Bro. Jarvis died just a few weeks following Dwight's death, that Dwight had already asked St. Peter if he could welcome Bro. Jarvis into that beautiful Heaven, as he was the one that made it possible for him being there.

The next Sunday after Dwight's funeral, his father and mother came to church and accepted Jesus and were baptized that night. I know there was rejoicing in heaven that night as there was in Una church.

After 11 years in service at Una, I was physically exhausted and began to pray that God would lead me as to what I was to do. The very next week I had a call from Dr. Fred Johnson at Grace Baptist Church that I had once pastored. He said he was in need of an Associate Pastor to lead the church in evangelism and help with other activities in the church. He wanted to know if I would accept that position?

I felt like it was God's answer to my prayer, as I would be doing what I loved most without having the responsibility of all the other duties involved in being the pastor. Well I accepted the position in 1982 and will get back to that experience when I come to that part of my life story.

My Ministry

Shelbyville Mills Baptist Church

I have completed both of my periods of service at Una, and now I will move on to the call that came to me from the Shelbyville Mills Baptist church in Shelbyville, Tennessee in 1959.

The pulpit committee came to Una, taped my message, went back, and played the message for the church. They extended a call without ever meeting me in person. I thought that was real strange, so I told them I would pray about that and let them know my answer.

After about two weeks of prayer and much thought I felt led to accept their call. I spent two wonderful years as their pastor, and many good things happened while I was there, and of course there were a few sad things that took place. The greatest blessing that took place was the first revival that I preached there after becoming pastor. There were 26 professions of faith, and the church had a continued growth period up until the time that I received a call from Rugby Hills Baptist church in Memphis and accepted their call to be their pastor in 1961. I felt that it was God's will, as my Dad had to take early retirement because of heart trouble, and I had not had the opportunity to be with him since his conversion experience. Even though I knew I would not get to see him very often, I knew I could see him more than I had in the past 20 years.

My Ministry

Rugby Hills Baptist Church

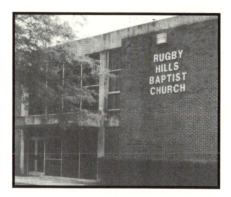

Several things happened in our transfer from Shelbyville to Rugby. It was a cold rain-soaked day when we loaded up a U-Haul, put our children and all the personal things in our van, and headed for Memphis. Nancy and I were in the front seat with the baby in her lap and lamps stuck in under feet. The other four children and loads of everything else were stuffed in the back.

It was very difficult for me to see anything through my back window for all the children and stuff. We had to stop for gas just outside of Frayser. While I was pumping gas, Mark slipped out of the car and went in the station. I had prepaid for the gas, so I got in the car and took off. After we had gone several miles, Nan shouted out loud that Mark was not in the car. He was only about five years old, and I was scared something would happen to him before I could get back. I turned around and drove back as fast as I could to the station and found him just standing on the corner leaning against a post. I asked him if he was scared, and he said, "No sir. I knew you would come back and get me."

Well that was a big relief, and we started on our way to Frayser. We arrived at the house where we were to stay at about 4:30 pm. The ladies of the church were there to meet us and had a big meal prepared. The U-Haul was being driven by one of the members of the church, and they arrived about five o'clock, unloaded the furniture, and we all sat down and enjoyed a wonderful meal together.

After the move, things began to happen that made me think that I had made a big mistake. When we began to look over our furniture we found several things had been broken, big rips in the couch, and some things we could not find. But all of this was minor compared to what I found when I went to the church and began to look things over.

I went into the classrooms and found empty food cans that were being used for ash trays in the rooms where the Bible was being taught by teachers that smoked, as well as some of the members of the class so I was told. There were three deacons, and they were all heavy smokers. The study where I was to do my preparation for sermons smelled like Reynolds and Reynolds Tobacco Company, and the church building was in real need of overhaul. After being there for about three weeks I knew something had to be changed if I was to stay there as pastor.

I wrote a letter to every member telling them I would be bringing a special message in two weeks and would like for all to be present. The church was packed, and I delivered the message that God had laid on my heart. After the message I told the people they must decide if they wanted a social club or a Bible believing church in order to let me know about staying as pastor. They voted to have the Bible believing church, and the three deacons and their families got up and left.

That night after I went home the three deacons had all called and said they were sorry about their decision, and they would be in church on Sunday. They went through the church with me and took out all of the ash trays and said they were ready to see the church take on knew life.

I think they were all surprised to see the big crowd that came to the service, and they were all back the next Sunday. Some of them had said the reason they stopped attending was because of the things that were going on in the church by those in leadership positions, and thought it was all because of their pastor that was doing the same thing as the members. Well, with this big step behind us we were ready to get the ball rolling in the right direction.

A Life of Miracles

The first thing was to draw up a new constitution and by-laws. We did, and it was accepted by the church, and we were on our way for Spiritual growth and physical growth. It was not long until we had completely out-grown all of our building and began to make plans for a building program. We had a difficult time finding a bond company that would help us as our budget was so small. But we finally were lucky enough to find one and got started.

We sold $150,000 worth of bonds, hired a contractor, and were on our way. Within a short period of time we were in our new building, and people were coming in so fast that we had to start planning for more space. The new people gave us the support that was needed to meet our budget needs.

There were many events that took place all during the time of the building program. The Home Mission Board called me and asked me if I would go to Chicago and preach a revival at a mission in North Chicago. It was a difficult decision, as we were in the middle of our building program, and decisions needed to be made every day. But I prayed about it and felt led to go.

A lady in our church named Mrs. Boston had terminal cancer. She called and asked me to stop by before I left. I thought she wanted me to have prayer with her about her condition, but she wanted me to try to see her sister there who had two daughters. None of the three were Christians. She gave me their address; I had prayer with her; and told her I would do my best. She thanked me and said she would be in prayer for my visit with them.

This was another miracle experience in my life while I was pastor at Rugby Hills. I caught the plane the next day and headed for Chicago. I arrived there about 3:00 p.m., and Bro. Smith, the pastor of the Mission was there to meet me. He was a very gracious young man, and we started on our 50 mile journey to his home in North Chicago. That time of the day was high traffic time, and it took us about one hour and a half to make the trip. There were dark clouds in the sky, and it looked as if we were going to have a real storm.

We went to one of the members house for a delicious meal before going to the church for the first service. We had just entered the building when the rain began to fall, and there were only six or seven people in the building. I thought I had made the wrong decision about taking the invitation of the Home Mission Board, but I felt impressed that it was God's will.

Well, the rain stopped for just a few minutes, and the people started entering the building. They must have been waiting for the rain to stop. In just a few minutes the room was full. About 65 people had come in. Then came the miracle. The last two people to come in were a young man named Agee, that I had not seen since I taught a Sunday School class in the living room of his father's home some 17 years ago; and the lady that came in with him—I found out after the service that night—was, hold your hat, yes you are right, it was the sister of Mrs. Boston that had asked me to try and see her. I almost fainted.

The Agee young man had seen a poster that told about the revival in the hall of the building where they both lived. When he saw my name he asked the lady if she would like to go with him to the revival. She told him that her sister had called her and told her about her pastor coming to Chicago and wished that I could meet him. If this is not God at work then what could it be?

They lived in a condo just a short distance to the O'Hare Air Port. You will see why I am telling you this on the next page. Remember I have told you that it was 50 miles from there to the church, and it was a very stormy night. That made it difficult for them to make the trip. But, I am sure God had heard the prayer of Mrs. Boston and was putting things in order to give her the answer to her prayers. Stay with me as we continue this true story that explains how God performs miracles.

The next night when we arrived at the church it was already pouring down rain with lightning flashing and thunder roaring. I thought no one would show up in that kind of weather, but to my surprise, the rain stopped, and the house was full once again. Then the last people to come in—yes you guessed it again—Mr. Agee, Mrs. Boston's sister, and her two daughters. I had hardly finished the message when all three were at the altar on their knees in prayer. I went down and found that they were seeking to know Jesus as their Saviour. God had sent his convicting Spirit upon them, I believe, because of the prayers of Mrs. Boston. They accepted Jesus, and several others came down for prayer. I was on cloud nine, as I could feel the power of God working out His plan to answer the prayers of Mrs. Boston.

I received a call from home that I was needed there the next day for some important decisions about the building construction I'd mentioned that from the pulpit before the message, and after the service I was invited by Mrs. Boston's sister to go home and spend the night with them, as they lived so close to the Airport. They would take me to the airport and pick me up the next afternoon, and bring me back to the church that night. I had never seen so many things happen in all of my ministry in just two days. Without a doubt that was a direct answer to prayer.

When we got to their apartment, I was so tired, but they kept me up until after midnight answering questions about the Christian life that God expected them to live. I was exhausted and just fell to sleep on the couch. They came in the next morning with a cup of coffee, and we jumped into their car and headed over to the airport. I got home before noon, went to the church, met the contractor, made the decision, was taken back to the airport, and was on my way back for the service that night. The lady and her two girls were there to meet me, and we were on our way to the church. The weather was simply beautiful. It just seemed to me that God was looking down from His throne in heaven and saying, "I hope you will always remember this revival, and that I will always be there when you follow my will."

I hope it will help all who read this book to know that Romans 8:28 is so true. "And we know that all things work together for good to them that love God, to them who are the called according to his purpose." Praise God from whom all blessings flow.

The six years that I had the privilege of serving the Lord at Rugby Hills were mixed with many different kinds of experiences. The first six months were very hard, but the rest of the time was wonderful. Even though we had some tough decisions to make, the Lord was there to see us through them all, and the work was blessed with a new building that would take care of 500 people for worship and Bible study. We had grown from 146 people to 465, and our fellowship was strong. Slowly, but very evident, the community was going through a changing experience, as several other communities were back in those days.

In 1967 I received a call from the Grace Baptist church in Nashville, asking me if I was going to be in my pulpit on the following Sunday. I told them I was, and they said they would be there, and would like to take me and my family out to dinner. Well, wheels started rolling, as

I knew another big decision was in the making. I knew that all of the pastors of Grace were doctors, and I was not even a practical nurse. I could not believe that they would be coming to hear me preach. Then I said maybe they just want me to preach a revival, but that thought was soon dismissed when I received a call the next day from Bro. Roberts who was chairman of the pulpit committee, and he told me they were looking for a pastor.

Well, they came, I preached, and we all went out for dinner. He asked me if I would come to Grace and preach for them. I told them that I had some important things going on right then that I needed to take care of and wish they would just keep looking for a pastor. I told them that I would be in revival at Rosedale Baptist church in Nashville the last week in February and maybe if they had not found a pastor by that time we could get together while I was there.

Now—on with my work at Rugby.

Well time moved on, and the revival time had come. I had not heard anything from them since they came to Memphis to hear me preach, but they were at the first service, and some of them were back every night. I was preaching through Sunday morning, and then I was to return home. They ask me if I would come and preach for them on that Sunday night, so I consented.

The church was full—over 700 people. When the service ended. I was escorted to the back, soon to be escorted back into the sanctuary. All the people were standing, and I was told, "There is your call to become our pastor."

I told the committee that I would be much in prayer about the call and would give them an answer as soon as I could feel God's will. In about two weeks I called them and told them that I would accept the call, but I could not come until school was out in June. They wanted me to fly back and forth on weekends until that time, but I just did not feel that was the right thing to do. I suggested they continue to look for a pastor. I was told that they were sure that God was in their call, and they would get supply preachers until I could come. Well that gave me the time I needed to help Rugby in their search for a new pastor and get some other things done before I left.

There were so many other experiences that I had there and feel like I should share two more before moving on to Grace. There was a man in our community called Big John. He was just that—about 275 pounds. John's wife was a member of the church. She prayed and asked for prayer for John several times.

Well he finally came to church and made his decision to accept Christ and said he wanted to be baptized in the river. I went down to the muddy Mississippi and took along a cane pole to probe the bottom and found a place where we could stand in about three feet of water. However, about two more feet the water dropped off to 20 feet. I was holding my breath and inwardly praying that Big John's feet would not slip, pull us both into that 20 feet of water, and send us floating down the muddy Mississippi.

I am sure the church members on the bank were also praying, as I had told them what the conditions were before I started the baptism. Well, once again the wonderful Lord was right there in the river with us, and everything went well. You could hear Nell, John's wife shout all over that river bank, jumping, clapping her hands, and praising the Lord. Now aren't you glad you had the chance to know about Big John?

I asked Big John why he wanted to be baptized in the river? His reply was, "I didn't think that little baptistry could hold enough water to wash all my sins away."

How is that for an answer? I told him later that it wasn't the water that washed away his sins, but the precious blood of Jesus. Just like in the song, "What can wash away my sins?Nothing but the blood of Jesus." Big John just smiled and said, "We got it done anyway." Big John had a very short time to practice the Christian life, as his big heart gave out, and the Lord came and took him to a better home. But praise the Lord, John was another direct answer to prayer. So let us never stop praying for those we know have never received Jesus as their Savior.

~~~~~~~~

I will always remember Bill Brown who was treasurer of the church when I went there. It didn't take long for the word to get around that Bill was stopping by the beer joint on his way to church and drinking with some of his friends. I began to pray for Bill and ask the Lord what we should do to help Bill see that his life style was not in keeping with the Christian life. It was just a few days later that I felt led to get a group of our men to go to the Brotherhood retreat at Camp Linden.

While we were there I was able to get alone with Bill one day, and sitting on a bench in the shade of a big oak tree I had a chance to talk with him about his life. We had not been talking very long until Bill started crying and told me that he was not saved and knew he was wrong in some of his actions and should not have an office in the church. Well, it was under that big oak tree kneeling in prayer that Bill gave his heart and life to Jesus. When we returned home Bill came forward in the church service and told the people that he was sorry for the things that were going on his life and ask them to forgive him. He said his desire now was to live for Jesus. He wanted to be baptized and come into the church as a believer, not just a member. He then said that he would give up his job in the church. One of the deacons stood up and said, "I believe that we should stand and let brother Bill know that he is forgiven and should continue to serve as church treasurer." And all stood with tears in their eyes to show they were proud of him for his decision. Bill continued taking care of the church money and never visited the beer joint again, but became a very dedicated Christian. He was asked to serve as a deacon but refused because he had been married and divorced. But he went on to serve the Lord in many other ways. One time he was asked to go and help witness in an area-wide crusade revival. He went, and the preacher assigned to his mission station got sick, and Bill brought the messages. Several people were saved, and Bill came home on cloud nine. Bill was a wonderful help to our church in so many ways, as were so many others: Brother Harber, our music director; Brother Shorty Comer, Chairman of the deacons and Bible teacher; Brother G.D. Jones, Bible teacher who was later called to be a preacher and pastored churches in Mississippi until his death. Brother Comer has also gone to his reward, but Brother Bill is still living at the age of 93.

There were so many others in the church that served the Lord in so many different ways. In fact, our membership had grown into a wonderful fellowship with a dedication to serve and honour our Lord, that even until this day we try to stay in touch. But so many have gone on to their reward that the number has become very small. We had reunions up until two year ago, but all that are left are getting too old to travel, so we had to stop getting together.

I must mention some that meant so much to the church in their unselfish giving of their time in service: Sonny Harber, who led our music and sang specials; my first convert, my brother-in law Robert "Shorty" Comer, Bible teacher, deacon, and handyman; G.D. Jones, deacon, Bible teacher, and later in life a preacher.

There were also three others that became preachers: Freddy Tubbs, Wayne Ferropulous, and Chuck Fowler. Chuck's wife Mary, was a dedicated Christian and prayed for Chuck often.

One day I had Chuck on my heart so much that I went to his barber shop to get a hair cut and witness to him. Before I left his shop, I pulled out a ticket to a brotherhood breakfast that we were having on the day our revival was to start. He took the ticket, but I really wondered if he would show up. Mary's prayers were answered. Chuck not only came to the breakfast, he stayed for the preaching service and came back on Monday night and accepted Jesus.

In a very short time, he answered God's call into the ministry, sold his barber shop, went to Seminary in Texas, and has pastored several churches. He's now retired but still preaching in churches in Mississippi when needed. Our Fellowship has been real close through the years and still is even today.

Not related to Rugby, but one of the dearest friends I have ever had through the years is Brother R.N. Coolidge. We have helped each other in several revivals. It was my joy to be with him in Comptche, California four times. He was the most talented person I have ever known, and it is sad for me to even write about him, as he is 92 years old and spends all of his days in a wheel chair. His wife Charlotte who has been a wonderful help-mate as she played the piano in churches where he pastored, and is still standing by his side. I could write a complete book about the experiences that we have had together through the years; but stay with me as we move on to Grace in Nashville.

My Ministry

Grace Baptist Church

Well school is out; Rugby has a new Pastor; and we are loaded and headed for Grace Baptist in Nashville. It is a very hot day in June as we travel on our way down I-40 with our five children. As you already know there were several pit stops on the way with seven people in the car, but we finally arrived in Nashville and had to sleep on the floor as our furniture would not arrive until the next day. But it was warm weather, and we had brought blankets and night clothes with us. The ladies of the church brought in our evening meal, so we would not have to fix anything.

The next day our furniture came, and we got all set up and ready for action. I went to the church and took my books to get them set up in my study. Mrs. Davis, the church secretary, helped me get things in order. She was such a gracious person and a tremendous help to me. She really knew how to handle the church office. The church was staffed with so many good people that were dedicated to the jobs they had to perform.

Bro J. Roy Bethune was minister of music and had a wonderful music program going for all age groups. There were about 50 well-trained choir members that blessed our hearts every Sunday with beautiful music. The children's choir would bless our hearts at times with a special program. I could never forget Brother J. Roy, as he would sit on the platform after leading the choir in the special music and almost fall out of his chair napping. He would shake his head, wake up, take out his comb, and put the 15 strands of hair back where they belonged. We got started off in the first service with a good response as several came forward to join the church. Of course, most of them were my family. But there were others who came also.

We continued to have new people come in almost every service, and our church was in the top ten in the state for baptisms. One year we had 43 come for baptism, and I preached 43 funerals that same year. I referred to some who had died as being asleep in Jesus, and one of my deacons said he saw several in the service that were asleep in Jesus. Oh well, you can't win every time.

We will continue with the activities while we were pastor at Grace. Don't put the book down now, as there is much more to come. Just turn the page, take another sip of tea, and keep reading. You just might find your name on the next page.

I had been pastor of Grace for only three weeks, when Brother Jimmy Morrisey, who was the treasurer of the church, came into my office and told me the bad news. Someone was taking money when counting, and he was pretty sure who it was. He had noticed that the money was always missing when the person that he thought might be guilty was counting the money. This did not happen with any of the other tellers. So I called the deacons in that evening and told them what was happening. We all agreed that we should contact the police department, and let them advise us about proper action. They suggested that we let them know the next time this person would be counting, and they would set up cameras in the attic and take pictures of what took place in the room where the tellers counted the money. Well, they came, and the tellers did not know what was going on, as the police had come in the day before and set up the cameras.

The next day there were three plain clothes policemen in the hall by the door of the room, waiting on a word from the men upstairs taking the pictures. Then all of a sudden the man came out of the room and went into the restroom. The men followed him and caught him taking the money out of his pockets, and they arrested him and took him to the police station. They kept him there until the next day when we could go down and make the decisions about the next step. He had taken several thousand dollars over a period of time.

Well all the men decided not to make it a church issue, but let him return home with the obligation to repay the money as soon as possible. He had bought several things that he began to sell and brought the money to the church. His children were out picking up drink bottles, and selling them to help pay the money back, and his wife had taken a job to help pay off the debt.

I am not using his name, because I don't want to hurt his family; and as far as I know, the church family never knew anything about the case, only the deacons. I do know that he was able to pay the money back, and was back in church, and even asked Brother Jimmy Morrisey if he could get back on the tellers committee. I am sure you must know what his answer was. Did you ever think anything like this could happen in the church? Well it did. I was just sorry it happened at Grace.

~~~~~~~~

After this experience with the man taking money from the collection while he was a teller, I was on a trip to Pickwick to meet some friends and go fishing. When I arrived at the Marina, I was told that a message had come for me to go to Baptist Hospital in Memphis. My Dad had been taken there with a massive heart attack. So I jumped in my car and took off for Memphis.

When I arrived at the hospital they had given Dad some medication. He was resting but awake. My brother Robert was there, and Dad looked up and said, "You boys go back home to your churches. I will be all right."

We had prayer with him and left to go back home. We had been home only a few hours, when we received a call to return to the hospital. But when we arrived Dad had already died. I stayed with Mother until things were taken care of about his arrangements, and then went back home to get my family and return to Memphis. We were there two days before the funeral service to help with things that needed to be done and see that Mother was going to be all right.

I was really surprised to see so many of the members of Grace that came to the funeral. I thought that nothing else could happen so quickly after being at Grace just a short period of time; but not long after getting back home I received word that my oldest brother Charles Jr. was flying eight people who were blind, and all members of the same family, to a hospital in Columbia, South America. The plane went down and had not been found. I contacted every one that I knew that might be able to give some advice about what we could do to find the plane, but nothing ever worked. Seven years later some hunters came upon the scene where the plane crashed, and a few personal things were sent back to his wife.

Well, life makes some swift turns sometimes that help us to realize the importance of staying in touch more often with those we love.

~~~~~~~~

Now it is time to move on into the next wonderful four years as pastor of Grace Baptist in Nashville.

Grace was well staffed with people who knew how to take care of the job they were responsible for, and that made my work much easer. Bro. Bill Crook, Chairman of Deacons; Jimmy Morrisey, Treasurer; Mrs. Christine Davis, Secretary; Mrs. Compton, Cook and many others served with humble dedication.

When I arrived Bro. J. Roy Bethune was Minister of Music and ready for retirement. It was a great loss to Grace when he left, but we were able to get Bro. Jerry Rankin to come. We enjoyed the time he was with us. Grace will always have a special place in my heart, as there were so many good things that happened while I was their pastor.

Nan, Steve, Bonnie, and Mark were all married there at Grace. Steve and Bonnie found their mates in the church family.

Nan Marie was married to Larry Lindsey, and they had two children: Kim and Allen. Kim is married to Toney Phillips, and they have two children: Bailey and Austin. Allen married Penny Ward, and they have two boys: Blain and Blake. They all live in Parsons, Tennessee.

Steve was married to Christy Rich, and they are still together. They had two children Cindy and John. Cindy LeMay married Allen Barnes and they have two children, Savannah and Christian. John LeMay married Lanna White, and they have three children. Lanna has two children, Evan.and Avery; and John has one son, Caleb.

Bonnie is married to William Brewer, and they have two boys, Brock and Barry.

Brock is married to Cynthia Fisher Brewer, and they have three children: Eli, Bella, and Sophia. Barry is married to Lana Brewer, and they have one adopted son, Jacob.

John Mark is married to Cindy Head LeMay, and they have three children: Josh, Heather, and Caleb. Josh is married to Mandy Maxwell Le May and has two boys: Levi Alexander, my name sake, and Luke. Heather is married to Eric Biggs. Caleb just graduated from high school.

Mary Lou was married to Terry Boyd, and they had two girls: Erin and Abbie. Erin is married to Matthew Goodall, and they have one daughter, Amelia. They live in Phoenix Arizona. Abbie is married to Brian Prescott, and they have one daughter, Mattie, and one on the way, Stella Carie. They live in Maine.

I know you must think your are reading the book of Numbers, but it is just our personal family up until this time. I feel sure there will be more later on down the line, as the last grandson and all the 17 greats grow up and get married. After you get through reading this family geneology, you will need to rest. Take another sip of that ice tea and maybe even take a nap before reading more.

LeMay Family

Hiram, Nancy, and LeMay Children

Nan Marie's Family

Steve's Family

Steve and Christy LeMay

Steve's Daughter Cindy Barnes and family

Steve's son Jon

Bonnie's family

Mark's Family

Mark's daughter Heather and Eric Biggs

Mark's son Josh and family

Mary Lou's family

My Ministry

Revival in New Zealand

We had come to that time in our society when change was taking place so fast that it affected our lives in many different ways. People were moving into and out of communities at such a high rate that life became unstable as decisions had to be made without having time to really give much thought to their actions. I had been pastor of Grace four wonderful years, but I could see that the church was going to have to make a move.

The Home Mission Board had contacted me about going to New Zealand for a revival in Taupo. The church had already voted to send my wife and I on a vacation trip to the Holy Land. I told them about the mission trip that had been offered to me, and they said, "Just do what you would like to do."

It was a real difficult decision, but I felt led to go to New Zealand for the Mission Revival. I had previously talked to the deacon body about what I felt like the church was facing in the near future. I would have to pray much about staying there at Grace.

We did go to Taupo, New Zealand and had a wonderful experience there as 12 Adults came to know Jesus as their Saviour, and several came on rededication. I was so glad that God had led me to make that decision, as it gave me time to think about my relationship with Grace.

While in Taupo, I had the experience of trout fishing one night in the Taupo River. The river was so clear that you had to fish at night as the fish could see you and move out to the deeper water, and we could not reach them. I was lucky and caught two real nice rainbow trout. A man in the church there cleaned them and cooked them for a going away dinner that they had for us. Mr. Story, the Mayor of Taupo, gave me a citation for the catch.

Brother Browning and his wife were such wonderful people, and we stayed in their home while we were there. When we came into Auckland, the fog was so heavy that we had to divert to Christ Church, which was 500 miles away. The pilot had told us that he would circle the airport for awhile to see if the fog would clear out, but we finally had to go to Christ Church and wait until the fog lifted. When we landed at Christ Church, we were greeted by men who entered the plane with tanks on their backs. They said they had to spray us with sheep dip to make sure we were not bringing in some disease that could kill their sheep.

After we were through with our sheep dip episode, they took us inside and fed us a delicious meal. We had lamb steak, mashed potatoes, green beans, and salad. They then brought out ice cream and cake. So we were ready to board the plane and head back to Auckland. It was about ten o'clock when we arrived, and the preachers were still there to meet us. Brother Browning and his wife came up to us and said we will head out for Taupo. Can you imagine what it is like for four people and four suit cases to be crammed into a Volkswagon and head out on 186 mile trip at 10: 30 at night after being in the air all day? Well take it from me, you don't want to have that experience.

When we arrived at the home of brother Browning, it took me about 15 minutes to get unwound from the luggage. I hurt all over. It was winter there, and we went in the house that had no heat and jumped into a bed with an electric blanket and pulled three quilts over us. We got about three hours sleep before breakfast. They never take their coats off in the house, as they don't have the money to pay a high electric bill. They operate on very low income. But every thing is much cheaper there than it is in the States.

One thing that surprised me was the way they buy food there. They get bread at the bakery, milk at the dairy, meat at the meat market, eggs at the poultry house, and staples at a corner store. They pay taxes according to the way they keep up their property, so everything there is kept nicely, even though the houses are very small.

It gave us a new appreciation of the things that we take for granted here in our country. We went to church the next day for our first service, and the little church was packed.

Everything was different from what we are used to in our churches. We were told that we should not leave the pulpit, as the pastor took care of the people that responded to the invitation. Children were not allowed to attend services at night, as they were to stay home and prepare for school. The children all dressed alike, and we never saw any of them acting up.

I was invited to speak at the school but was restricted from inviting children to the revival. The Head Master wanted me to speak on Martin Luther King, but I told him my mission was to speak about the King of Kings. He said that would be all right but not to give an invitation for the children to make decisions.

We had some wonderful experiences while there in Taupo. Twice a day we went into different homes at their ten o'clock and two o'clock tea times to share pictures, answer questions, and have a short message. They always served some of the good cookies and cakes they had made. Some of the ladies that came to the tea times came to the services at night, and some received Jesus as their Saviour. They had a waiting period for those who came for baptism. They had to attend classes for six weeks before they could be accepted for baptism. One lady wrote me a letter and said she had finished her classes, was now ready for baptism, and was so happy.

We had a chance one day to go over the mountain to Rotorua and visit the area with all the hot bubbling springs. We were told by the guide as we walked the narrow, winding path by the steaming water, that some times they would lose someone who got to close to the edge, and they would disappear. That was pretty scary but a very new experience for us.

Some of the houses in that area had springs under their houses, and they piped the hot water into their houses for heating and taking showers. I said when we were through with our tour, that I was glad we had hot water heaters back home. We found it to be pretty hard to find the time for rest, as the people wanted to sit and talk for hours after the nightly service. I have never experienced people as hungry for the Gospel as they were in Taupo.

Leaving Taupo, we went to Australia and spent two nights there with some very nice people who had opened their doors for us. We also found people so open for the Gospel and full of questions.

A Life of Miracles

From there we went to Hong-Kong, where we had time to visit some of the gift shops and take a ride on a tour boat. It was on this boat that I had the privilege of sharing the Gospel with one of the tour guides, and she received Jesus. Her name was Alice Hoo-Wong. I gave her the little New Testament, and she said she was going to share it with one of the boys on the boat.

We saw poverty as I have never seen it before, with families living in cardboard huts on the side of a hill and children in small boats begging for money. One of our young preachers broke down crying as he saw the conditions that people had to live in. That young black preacher said he was going back to his congregation in Mississippi and tell them to stand up and sing God Bless America, and he didn't want to hear any body complain about being poor. We were told that some of the people that lived on boats never came on land but lived and died on the boat. It was very hard for me to realize that people had to live like animals.

When we got back from the boat trip, we boarded the airplane and headed for Japan to attend the Baptist World Alliance. That was a real experience. We could hear delegations from Russia yelling to the top of their voices about the way they were being treated in their country. Many were being killed and some put in prison. It seemed that any minute there would be a real battle started inside the convention hall. Security officers came in and stopped the noise, but it was real frightening.

We were in Tokyo for three days, and there were gun shots being fired in the hotel next to the one where we stayed. We went out shopping the second day and had some real funny experiences. Some of the shops that we visited, where people our age were waiting on customers, acted as if they did not want to help us. I thought it was because we were the age of the ones we fought in World War II, and they were still mad at us for winning the war. But a younger English speaking person came in and told us that the others were not able to communicate, so they just sat and would not even move.

In some shops it was really hard to find some one who could understand English enough to wait on us. On our last day there we took the fast train up to the top of Neckore Mt. and had dinner in a huge restaurant over-looking a beautiful lake. We ordered trout, and they brought out a trout on a plate that had been cooked head and all and had not been cleaned. I ate part but had to stop when I found the insides had never been removed. That was one more experience. I thought what I had already gulped down was going to come back up before we got to the bottom of that mountain traveling 200 miles an hour. Well, it was time to board the plane again and head for the good old USA.

My Ministry

Back to Grace

We had only been home a short time when I received a call from Una Baptist Church. They had just gone through a big split, lost their pastor, and their membership had dropped down to less than 150. They ask me to come and help them. It was a real answer to my prayers about God's will for my life. I have already given account of the 11 years that I spent there before going back to Grace in Nashville where I will continue to tell about the six wonderful years that I spent there with Dr. Fred Johnson and the gracious people of Grace.

My position was Associate Pastor, Bible teacher, and Teacher of E.E. (Evangelism Explosion). I went to the First Baptist Church of Oklahoma City to attend a study course in E.E. Dr. James Kennedy, Pastor of the Coral Ridge Presbyterian Church in Ft. Lauderdale Florida, was the founder of this very successful program that was used to help many people come to know the Lord as their Saviour. I found it to be very helpful and successful when we used it at Grace. Teaching that class was a real joy. We experienced the privilege of seeing others come to know Christ, find answers to their spiritual needs, and become better witnesses for their Lord.

I had several other opportunities to serve the Lord there, as I did a lot of hospital visitation and made visits to nursing homes and people who were sick but still at home. I would also preach for Dr. Johnson on several occasions. That included some funerals and weddings. Dr. Johnson and I had a wonderful six years of Christian fellowship together. Bro. Jerry Rankin was our minister of music at that time, and we all enjoyed our fellowship together. We acted like we were characters on Sanford & Sons and would have fun acting out our parts at different times.

As time moved on, Nancy was having health problems, so I knew I would have to cut back on my activities. I was contacted by Bro. Dickens who was a deacon of a mission church in Pleasant View, Tennessee. He said that they needed someone to come and lead them in getting organized and help them get into a building program. I accepted the challenge on a part time relationship that turned full-time in just a short while. We managed to set up the organization and get into a building in two years. The church had about 125 members at that time.

My Ministry

Pleasant View Baptist Church

There was a lot of work to be done, setting up the organization, and getting into a building. When I went there they were meeting in a classroom at the school with pictures of animals all over the walls and only space for about 30 people. David Bailey and his wife Ginnie had given property for a church to be built. We had plans made with the help of the Sunday School Board, and a man in the church named Percy Black accepted the job of overseeing the building project. With the help of the members, both men and women, work was under way.

There were a few things that had to be done by contractors such as plumbing, roofing, and electrical, but most of the other work was done by the members of the church. It was my good pleasure to build most of the furniture including the kitchen cabinets, pulpit, communion table, and hall table for the vestibule. I also built two chairs for the platform and the rail in front of the choir.

Paul Smith and I laid the floor in the vestibule and also helped with the sheet rock. Bro. Jacobs was a real help in putting up the sheet rock, and the ladies did most of the painting. Bro. Lando Barnett was the man that took on the job of hauling the church pews from a Church of

Christ who sold us their pews. That was a very hard job, but they fit in very well with our building.

It was a great day of celebration when we were able to move from the school into that nice new building in 1992. By that time Nancy's health had become much worse, and I knew I would have to make another move.

In the late fall of 1992, I was contacted by Grace Baptist in Tullahoma to come and be their interim pastor. Another answer to prayer. It was then that I resigned the church at Pleasant View and went into semi-retirement. We sold our home in Pleasant View, bought a farm house with five acres of ground in Winchester, stayed at the Grace Baptist Church in Tullahoma for about a year. We moved into the house in Winchester, and Nancy's condition continued to get worse day by day. For the next seven years, I was able to take short interims for five different churches, only preaching three times a week, and doing no church work. By 1996 Nancy was going through such a hard time that I could no longer take any church work. She was in and out of the hospital several times and finally made her last trip September 20th. She went to her heavenly home September 28, 1998.

My Ministry

Revivals and Convention Work

In the home of Cathy Wallace during the Marble Plains Revival

From the early years of my ministry until 1998, I was very active in holding revivals and had the privilege of preaching revivals in twelve different states including four in California, three in Georgia, two in Alabama, and about 50 in Tennessee. And one in Taupo, New Zealand. It was my pleasure to preach the message at several Evangelistic Conferences in our state. It was with joy that I accepted the opportunities to serve on several boards and committees in the TBC and SBC across the years.

A real surprise came when I was elected to serve the Tennessee Baptist Convention as second Vice President in 1975. Bro. Charles Fowler, my son in the ministry, made the nomination. All of these experiences took time, but I really enjoyed them all, and I am sure that I got more out of serving these different jobs than I could have meant to their progress. I so well remember in the '50's and '60's that most revivals lasted for two weeks. We would spend the week before the revival having prayer meetings in different homes and inviting people to come that were not attending church anywhere. It always resulted in some of them coming to the revival and some receiving Jesus as their Savior.

Things have changed so much in the past 20 years that it is hard to get people to come out for five services. Some churches now only have what they call one day revivals, and some have quit having revivals at all. Some of the greatest revivals that I can remember back through the years was when we had all night prayer before the revival started; and in some cases that is where the revival would start, as some would get saved while trying to pray for revival. That is what happened to me in 1946. It also happened to Sonny Harber at Rugby Hills in Memphis and others that I know about in different churches.

Well this brings us to the end of our ministry up through 1998. Since then it has just been preaching whenever I have an open door. I started a Bible class here in the complex where we live, and it is touching the lives of several people.

May God add his blessings to all who read this life story. My earnest prayer is that some might be touched enough to respond to God's call to serve Him.

Teaching bible study at Lenox members

Bible study group

Epilogue

I am writing this part of my personal life with much prayer that it might be a help to someone who is going through the same kind of experience that I had.

There came the time in my life when the mountains of loneliness were too high for me to climb. The valleys were too filled with despair for me to walk through. The nights were too dark for me to see ahead. And the days so filled with questions that needed answers, that I had to turn to the Word of God to receive the guidance that He had promised me in Proverbs 3: 6.

The first scripture that came to my mind was Psalm 23. The assurance came to me that like David, the Lord was my Shepherd, and I felt that he was going to lead me over the mountain of loneliness and through the valley of despair; turn on His light in the dark nights; and answer my questions that kept coming to me in the long days.

My mind then turned to the promises that God had made in His word. John 10:10 came to my mind, and I read it over and over again.

"I am come that they might have life, and that they might have it more abundantly."

It was not very long until my phone rang. Dr. Darrell Craft called to remind me that I was to preach for him on the second Sunday in October. I went to Shelbyville and preached for him. While I was there, it just seemed that the Lord was telling me to ask one of the ladies to have dinner with me. I did, and a few days later I went to her home and took her out to dinner. We went out several times and seem to enjoy each other's company; and in February I asked her if she would consider getting married. So Mrs. Lois Canter became my wife. She had five girls, and I had five children. That was a crowd.

We had 4 years filled with travel and happy experiences, then cancer returned and took her life. So I was back where I had been before. I began to pray that God would again lead me in the decisions that I needed to make. I called a preacher friend of mind and told him that I was so lonely and asked him to be in prayer for me to find God's will. Dr. Hubbard and his wife Fay became very concerned and promised to pray for me. Just a few days later, Fay called and told me about a lady who was a member of the church where Dr. Hubbard had pastored in Chattanooga. They were real dear friends.

Fay told me that she had called her and ask her if she could give me her phone number. I learned later that the lady told her that she wasn't interested, as all men were just looking for a nurse and a purse. Fay called her back and assured her that I was not looking for either one and told her all the good things she could think of about my life, as she had known me every since she was a little girl.

Well about two weeks later Fay called her again, and asked if she could just give me her number so I could call and just see what would happen. She told Fay that she had been praying about it, and that she thought it would be all right to let me call. Well, I did; and I asked her if I could come and take her out for lunch, and she said okay.

I asked my daughter Bonnie to go with me, and we loaded up and took off to Chattanooga to meet Mrs. Jessie Ruth Hearn on Brandermill Street. I will never forget what she said, as we walked in her front door. "What you see is what you get."

I liked what I saw and began to make several visits across that mountain until I finally convinced her that she needed to change her name to Jessie Ruth LeMay. I was 79 at the time and said to her one day, "Jessie, had you rather marry a man 79 or one who is 80?"

My birthday is July 31. That was in March. She said, "Let's set July 17."

So we were married in the home of Dr. Hubbard on July 17, 2004; and we have had eight wonderful years together come July 17. We both believe without any doubt, God worked another miracle in bringing us together. Jessie has three fine sons: Michael, Steve and David. They stay in constant touch with their mother every day. My five children all love her very much and enjoy being around her.

With our seventh anniversary behind us, we are looking forward to July 17, 2012 so we can celebrate our eighth year together, thanking God each day for Dr. Hubbard who has gone to his heavenly reward, and for his wife Fay who is our dear friend.

Hiram with Jessie and Sons

Hiram and Jessie with Mike

Chuck and Mary Fowler

The Last Page

I could not think of closing this book without thanking my Loving Lord for giving me the privilege of having the very best people in all the world to spend my life on earth with, and the blessings they have brought into my life. It would take all year, and then some to try to name each one by name, but there are some that I feel that I must say a special word of thanks to; Some who have been a special blessing in my ministry there have been those that have helped me so much, and made my service to my Lord a real blessing. Preacher friends. Bro. Raymond Cooledge, Charles Fowler, Jack Hice, Bob Mitchel, and my pastor Dr. Larry Yarborough. Members of churches I have pastored that have been a special blessing. Ollen Crowder, Marvin Jarvis, Bill Brown, James Waller, Hilary Dawson, Robert Comer, Bill Brown, Bill Crook, James Morrissey, David & Ginnie Bailey, Bob & Pat Boswell and their family that have been such a blessing in so many ways. Casey & Tracy and their family Lilly & Hudson. WOW ! The many good things they have done to bless our lives. Don & Ruth Spurgon, George Furgerson, Mark & Kathy Wallace family. Doc. & Sue Prince. Friends not related to the churches I have served. Jim & Gloria Bible, Frank & Martha Bird, Leland & Evalyn Sizemore, Ken & Fay Hubbard, Frank & Lyn Drewrey, Winston & Betty Radolph, Don & Loretta Brown. Wert Campbell, teacher, and bible study members. This could go on forever so must stop here. I love all of my friends and realize that I know so many because of Jesus bringing us together.

Reverend Raymond Coolidge and Charlotte

The Boswell Family
This family has meant so much to me in so many different ways
in my later years that they feel like family.

Casey and John Boswell and H.A.

Pat and Bob Boswell

Families from Rugby

Dorris, Mike, and Bill Herron

Denise and Bonnie Hearn

Jim and Gloria Bible

THE END